Skiing Cross Country

Skiing Cross Country

by
Ned Baldwin

McGRAW-HILL RYERSON LIMITED

Toronto   Montreal   New York   London
Sydney   Auckland   Johannesburg   Düsseldorf
Mexico   Panama   São Paulo   Singapore   New Delhi

SKIING CROSS COUNTRY

ISBN 0-07-082490-8

2   3   4   5   6   7   8   9   0   THB   5   4   3   2   1   0   9   8

Printed and bound in Canada

Canadian Cataloguing in Publication Data

Baldwin, Edward R., 1935–
  Skiing cross country

Bibliography: p.
ISBN 0-07-082490-8 pa.

1. Cross-country skiing. I. Title.

GV854.9.C7B3452   796.9'3   C77-001560-3

About the People who Made this Book

Ned Baldwin is the author of *The Cross-Country Skiing Handbook* (Pagurian Press 1972; Revised edition 1973) *The Beginner's Guide to Cross-Country Skiing* (Greywood Publishing Ltd. 1972) and *The Family Guide to Cross-Country Skiing* (Pagurian Press 1976). He has been active in all types of skiing for nearly 40 years. He was a keen competitor in both nordic and alpine events throughout his school years and in 1971 and 1972 was a member of the winning 4 man touring team in the Canadian Ski Marathon, an annual 90 mile, 2 day event attracting over 3000 competitors. He is also an experienced expedition mountaineer having participated in the 1967 Canadian Centennial Expedition to the St. Elias Mountains in the Yukon Territories and has led his own expeditions to the Canadian Rockies, North Cascades, Mt. Ranier, Wind Rivers, the Volcanoes of Mexico, and the Cordillera Blanca in Peru. When not skiing or climbing, he is white water canoeing or scuba diving. In his real world Mr. Baldwin is an architect. The CN Tower in Toronto, Harvard Graduate School of Design in Cambridge, Massachusetts and the Port of Miami Passenger Terminal in Miami, Florida are among his architectural accomplishments.

Principal photographers for the book include Mate Lenard of Wild Leitz Canada and Conrad Stenton of Ernst Leitz Ltd. Mate and Conrad spent many hours trudging through snow with their Leica cameras capturing the action.

Principal illustrator for the book was Bonnie Sheppard, a ski instructor, and as such, dedicated to portraying accurately all manoeuvers on skis.

Many others have contributed to the production . . . Tim and Peter Griffin as tireless subjects in numerous photos and Sandy Budden as writer/editor of Chapter 10 and Pamela Harley as the courageous typist.

DEDICATION

This book has an ulterior motive. It is
dedicated to my fanatic desire to see
all those who take up cross-country
skiing discover the added dimension
of skiing off-the-trail, in deep snow,
and most importantly, down hills. To
me this dimension is the greatest form
of skiing, but one which, unfortunately,
most new enthusiasts are missing.

TABLE OF CONTENTS

PREFACE

Most of us live in a world where we are highly insulated from the natural environment around us, so much so that we are barely conscious of it. Even when we make an effort to contact it, we invariably bring the trappings of our "civilized life" along. Camping is done from a trailer, fishing from a power boat, and even hiking, only on a trail, only in an established park.

Most of my life I have searched for ways and means of stripping away this insulation and discovering the wilderness of a first-hand basis. To me there is no substitute for direct exploration, independent of organizations and the rules, timetables, and procedures which seem to go with them.

Cross-country skiing has often provided me with the perfect medium in which to find this independence. Just as one can leave man's civilization behind within minutes by paddling down a river away from a highway, similarly a skier is immediately in another world the moment he leaves the trail. The ease with which one can move on skis while still being totally conscious of one's surroundings is quite unique among experiences. If the snow is new and very soft it is possible to move almost totally without sound. One often runs up on game in these conditions. When the snow is older and more coarse, the scraping sound of the skis is fascinating to animals and while they are spooked by the sound at first, they often stop and return in curiosity to see what it might be.

So all of this tells you a bit about why I am addicted to cross-country skiing. There are other reasons too . . . . I love the sensation of moving fast with control. Just as with a racing car one's survival is one hundred percent dependent upon one's timing and precision. The skier descending the steep hill in the woods is totally reliant on his ability to anticipate his path through the trees, and to control his motion so that it conforms to it. While I am a keen alpine skier as well, somehow the concentrations of skiers on the slope, the groomed snow, and the similarity of the track which one tends to take on each run, make it far less rewarding.

My primary interest in Cross-Country Skiing then, is in skiing down hills and exploring the winter wilderness away from the trail. For others, the challenges will lie in exploring the limits of their bodies by running on a race course. Some will be content to slide in the tracks of others on developed trails. All who try cross-country skiing will develop one of these specializations. My hope in this book is to expose all cross-country skiers, or prospective skiers, to the sport's diversity.

CHAPTER ONE
THE DIFFERENT KINDS OF CROSS-COUNTRY SKIING

Figure 1.2 An ideal area for a geschmossel start.

This book will deal with the techniques and equipment required for all types of cross-country skiing. It will not discuss alpine or downhill skiing which since the 1930s has been quite a separate sport. It will also not deal in depth with the more subtle techniques and training procedures required for cross-country racing, nor will it cover the other half of nordic competition, jumping. Downhill skiing is a vast subject in itself and competitive cross-country skiing and ski jumping are subjects for others far better qualified than I.

I have practiced cross-country skiing for over 35 years in all kinds of terrain and with equipment ranging from racing to ski mountaineering weights. Over the years I have seen many people confused by this variety; perplexed at the need for different equipment and techniques in different terrain and snow conditions. In this chapter I will attempt to clarify the need for this diversity in the hope that the reader will be able to decide for himself or herself what form of cross-country skiing he or she is interested in.

COMPETITION

Since the well-televised Olympics in Innsbruck the general public has become increasingly conscious of competitive cross-country skiing as a major sport. Now many people are becoming interested in challenging the traditional domination of the sport by the Scandinavians, Eastern Europeans, and the Russians.

There is no more demanding sport than cross-country ski racing. The only activities which, in my judgement, rival it would be sports such as water polo or soccer where one is constantly exerting maximum physical effort. The importance of technique in cross-country ski racing is paramount. Only at the international or world class competition levels is technique for all the racers virtually the same and the sport once again resolves itself to a battle between various levels of fitness. At the more amateur levels the experienced skier and the one who has developed the smoothest striding technique is inevitably the winner. Twenty-five years ago, when I was competing on a university ski team, the technique for virtually every racer was so poor that any competitor of Scandinavian origin who had grown up in an environment where technique was actually taught, meant certain victory for him. Today some North Americans have developed excellent techniques, but it will still take years before they can *consistently* be competitive at the world class levels. Both in Canada and the United States the national nordic team members have many Finnish, Norwegian and Swedish names.

Figure 1.3 In the first moments the pre-start tensions begin to evaporate.

I think that most people today, their first exposure to cross-country skiing coming from watching competition on television, are naturally attracted to the super light-weight racing equipment. Since this equipment is only suited for trail skiing they find themselves skiing only on prepared tracks. In my judgement this has often proved a disappointment for many people who are not competitively inclined. It takes a certain sadistic and masochistic nature to really enjoy an all out "thrash" on cross-country skis. Unless one has excellent technique this is invariably what racing becomes.

Competitive cross-country skiing utilizes the lightest and most fragile equipment; very light pin bindings, superlight and narrow double cambered skis, featherweight boron fibre reinforced plastic poles with butterfly baskets which will not drag in the snow, very light clothing, and ventilated gloves. It is the epitomy of efficient travel on skis over distance. It demands a broken trail or prepared ski track

simply to use the equipment. If moving fast over long distances and testing your endurance holds fascination for you, you will enjoy cross-country racing. It is a superb physical challenge. Many ski touring centers now offer groomed racing trails for training purposes. The number of racing events grows each year providing more and more opportunities for any skier interested in this aspect of cross-country.

Figure 1.4 Brief moments of man-to-man competition.

Figure 1.5 No. 117 is in the best position among these competitors and appears to be having difficulty in passing No. 89 and No. 56.

International Classes of Competitors
As set by the F.I.S.
(Fédération Internationale de Ski)

MEN

CLASS	AGE ON JANUARY 1	MAXIMUM RACE LENGTH
Senior	21 and over	F.I.S. - 50 km, otherwise unlimited
Senior	20	20 km
Junior	18 and 19	15 km
Younger Junior	16 and 17	10 km
Older Boys	14 and 15	5 km
Younger Boys	12 and 13	3 km
Small Boys	11 and under	2 km

WOMEN

CLASS	AGE ON JANUARY 1	MAXIMUM RACE LENGTH
Senior	18 and over	F.I.S. - 50 km otherwise 35 km touring
Junior	16 and 17	5 km
Older Girls	14 and 15	5 km
Younger Girls	12 and 13	3 km
Small Girls	11 and under	2 km

North American class breakdowns are *not* consistent with the above. Many senior classes are differentiated into numerous veteran categories up to age 40 and over. Competition is extremely keen in the 30-40 year age groups and even older.

Figure 1.7

Figure 1.6 A cup of Ambrosia.

* Canadian Ski Association, 333 River Road, Ottawa, Ontario. Tel. (613) 746-3324.

United States Ski Association, 1726 Champa, Suite 300, Denver, Colorado 80202 Tel: (303) 825-9183.

Cross-country ski racing is divided into *sanctioned events:* those recognized by the national ski organizations and open only to registered competitors; and *popular events* open to any interested member of the public.

To become a registered competitor it is only necessary to contact the nordic committee of your national ski association * and pay a nominal sum for a competitor's card. Your racing classification will be established only after you have participated in a season's races. Obtain a calendar of racing events and plan to attend as many as possible. Only by trying it out can you really know what cross-country racing is like!

Popular racing events are generally called touring races and the emphasis is usually on covering a distance rather than making a fast time. However, how can any event where everyone starts together be anything but an all out race? Most of the popular events have racing classes as well, so just because you have become a registered competitor and the race isn't listed on your calendar of sanctioned events, don't stay away! The popular events have many classifications allowing children, families, and father/son, mother/daughter, brother/sister, grandfather/grandson combinations to compete for individual awards. Skiers in these events often run on touring skis and the whole scene is much less intense. Such races are a lot of fun and an excellent way for an adult or child to find out what cross-country competition is like.

Sanctioned races are usually 5, 15, 30, or 50 kilometers (3 to 31 miles) in length, while popular events range from an all out dash of 2.5 km to the 100 mile (2 day) Canadian Ski Marathon from the Laurentians north of Montreal to the Gatineau Hills outside Ottawa. Sanctioned races are run on a single ski track with each racer starting individually at one minute intervals. Popular events usually require a mass, or "geschmossel" start, due to the very large numbers of competitors. The 42 km Engadin Marathon between the villages of *Maloja and Zuoz* passing through *St. Moritz* in Switzerland recently attracted over 15,000 competitors! (Figure 2-8).

In a geschmossel start all competitors mass behind the starting line and spread out in a mad dash across a lake or large field at the starting gun. It is a scramble to get into the lead at once so that you are not blocked by other racers when the track narrows at the end of the open starting area. If you do not get into the lead you are doomed to have to attempt passing perhaps hundreds of skiers on the trail which often involves tiring detours into deep snow. Racing etiquette demands that if you are overtaken by another skier who calls "track", that you move entirely off the trail allowing him to pass. Often, however, a racer will refuse to move off because there is someone immediately ahead of him who refused to move, and ahead of him, etc.

International Events

Courses are as prescribed by the F.I.S.,
(Fédération Internationale de Ski)

COURSE	TOTAL ELEVATION GAIN
5 km Women's	150 - 200 meters
10 km Women's	250 - 350 meters
10 km Men's	300 - 450 meters
15 km Men's	450 - 600 meters
30 km Men's	750 - 1000 meters
50 km Men's	1200 - 1500 meters

North American events often deviate from these standards. Courses in flat country, of course, do not have the elevation gain prescribed and others in mountainous terrain often have far more.

In addition to the normal running events, relays, the biathalon, and the combined events are usually held in major competitions. These are as follows:

Relays:
Three or four men run ten kilometers each and four women run five kilometers each. Courses are laid out with two parallel tracks and the race is an all-out sprint from start to finish.

The Biathalon
This is a twenty kilometer cross-country race with four men each running five kilometer legs and shooting at targets twice enroute. The racer carries a rifle and is scored for marksmanship as well as total team elapsed time.

The Combined
This is a fifteen kilometer running event combined with the sixty meter jumping competition, the winner having the highest placing in both events. It is an especially coveted event in Norway at the annual Holmenkollen competition. In 1968, an American, John Bower, won this event, a spectacular achievement.

Figure 1.8

Cross-country racing is truly a participative sport, great fun only for the competitor himself. As a spectator sport it has to rank even behind yacht racing. Yet surprisingly in Scandanavia where it is so ingrained in the life of every school child, large numbers of spectators do turn up and spread out all along the trail on skis to cheer the racers on. In North America the only spectators one usually sees are at the finish line or at one or two check points along the way. The olympic events in Innsbruck were quite exciting to watch on television because of the use of multiple cameras covering several parts of the race course simultaneously.

Due to sequence starting it is difficult for the spectator to tell which competitor is winning. If you see a high bib number passing a low number it generally means he is faster but it is hard to have any more accurate appreciation of where he may stand. As a competitor oneself, watching a cross-country race for technique can be invaluable. I recommend skiing out along the course to one of the most grueling hills to see how the really good ones climb. Steep descents with sharp corners are fun to see too, but the action is so very brief there. On a good long hill you are more apt to see the men separated from the boys. The finish line is quite interesting especially after a long race where there is a lot of difference in the condition of the runners.

Figure 1.9 A lunch and sunbathing stop. Highlights of any trail tour.

If competition as an individual is your thing, where you and only you, control the results of your performance, then cross-country racing is very likely for you. I have always enjoyed it because it lasts a decent length of time. As an alpine ski competitor I was always frustrated by the fact that a slalom race only lasted a minute and one half or so. It took me all of that time simply to get rid of the butterflies in my stomach which had concentrated there after hours of studying the course and waiting to start! I always did stupid things like forgetting to breathe which usually brought disaster to my performance. In cross-country, on the other hand, one has substantial time in which to work out those butterflies. They are still there, of course. Pre-race tensions always develop as you worry about your wax job and watch the smooth technique of your competition warming up. Once out of the starting gate, however, it is very much a race with yourself except for those brief man-to-man challenges when a better guy goes by you and you try to keep on his tail or vice versa. Even a spill is not an irrecoverable disaster to your end performance. Frustration over having the improper wax can often evaporate as the wax performance improves further into the race. As the kilometer markers click by, and you really get moving, nothing compares with the thrill of that last sprint towards the finish and the delicious exhaustion afterwards.

Figure 1.10 Stuck in the ruts of thousands of skiers? This overdressed fellow will hardly experience the freedom of cross-country.

RECREATIONAL TRAIL TOURING

Perhaps the bulk of people taking up cross-country skiing automatically fall into the category of recreational trail tourers. They purchase equipment which is somewhat heavier and more durable than racing equipment; skis which are wider, perhaps up to 45 to 50 millimetres at the shovel; bindings which are slightly more rugged but normally of the pin type; and poles. They head off to their nearest advertised ski touring center where they take lessons and learn to ski. The trail tourer is dependent on a broken track, hence the requirement for these skiers to find "places" to go cross-country skiing where there are trails already prepared for them. Recreational trail touring also constitutes the bulk of cross-country skiing in Scandanavian countries. In my judgement the vast majority of people taking up cross-country skiing today are finding themselves in this category without the benefit of knowing what alternatives there

Figure 1.11 Striking out away from the trail into the untracked snow.

are. They may know about competitive skiing and not be interested in that, but they invariably have little or no knowledge of the other alternatives. Trail touring is best done with light or standard touring skis and generally in relatively flat country. Trail touring is usually popular in areas which are somewhat developed. Carrying food or backpacking for overnight stays is not an aspect of this type of skiing. It is generally done for short periods at a time and one can return to one's car, hotel, or base lodge at the conclusion of the tour.

Trail touring unfortunately implies crowds; and where the trails are maintained there is often a charge for using these trails. This is something I'm afraid I have an inborn resistance to but unfortunately if men and machines are involved in making a place enjoyable for skiing, it is going to have to cost someone some money. All too often the "groomed" trails amount to an expanse of packed slope where it is difficult to control one's skis at all. Where the trail has been properly grooved with regulation ski tracks, (Figure 1.10) often the sheer number of skiers makes it difficult to make time. Sometimes too, the grooved tracks have been made for extremely narrow racing skis or light touring skis and you find that your skis won't fit the track!

I apologize for my obvious bias against packed trail, "organized" trail touring. It is the result of years of seeing newcomers to the sport start in this way and never discover its other dimensions which I find so much more interesting. For the city dweller who wants to ski after work, there is little alternative to skiing on a packed snow surface. Within hours of a snow storm that is all that remains in a city. Now if that same city dweller were to rise at dawn after a snowstorm what pleasures he would find on those same park slopes and trails!

DEEP SNOW TOURING

This type of skiing is the other dimension to which I have referred. It is skiing away from a broken trail, independently through the woods, across fields and up and down hills. Here one is not dependent on other skiers or any preparation of the snow. In my judgement, it is the type of cross-country skiing which would have the widest appeal to families and most individuals if they were exposed to it. Deep snow touring requires slightly wider, heavier, and sturdier equipment than for trail skiing. This equipment is difficult to find and it is for this reason that so few people practice it. The advantages of not relying on a trail are numerous. First, our landscape can absorb a multitude of skiers without congestion if they ski independently. Secondly, the costs which inevitably come with development of ski "areas", groomed trails, traffic congestion, and the like are completely avoided. Thirdly, the enjoyment of the undisturbed winter landscape for photography, bird and animal track watching, and simply listening to its beautiful quiet, is vastly enhanced. And fourthly, and perhaps most importantly, off-the-trail touring allows for exciting downhill runs with control, something usually denied the trail skier.

Figure 1.12 A hidden field awaiting Telemarks.

My bias in favour of this kind of skiing will permeate this whole book. There will be those who say I exaggerate the need for sturdier equipment and that they manage quite well in deep snow with their lightweight gear. This may well be true for some, but for most I know it is not. The light touring skis which so totally dominate the cross-country ski industry have a number of failings when it comes to deep snow. First, their narrow width (45-60 millimeters measured at the shovel) does not allow enough planing effect or flotation in soft snow. Secondly, their sharp turned-up tips tend to "plow" the snow, slowing down the skier. Thirdly, their high flexibility makes their response extremely "soft" in firm snow in downhill descents. These problems pertain whether they are made of wood or fiberglass; whether they are of the wax or no-wax type. Actually, the new technology being used for skis offers all sorts of opportunities for producing superb deep snow skis, but so far, few of the manufacturers are doing it.

17

Figure 1.13 If you like to ski you will eventually seek out the mountains.

So these equipment problems, and the big business promotion of cross-country skiing on trails at resorts, both conspire to make deep snow touring impractical. I write this book principally in the hopes that its readers will persevere and discover this exciting new dimension.

MOUNTAIN SKIING OR SKI MOUNTAINEERING

If you love the mountains and live near them it is inevitable that you will want to visit them in the winter. This is when they are in their full glory; most threatening, and most challenging. Ski ascents and descents are some of the most thrilling experiences in the mountains. Skis enable one to cross terrain in much greater safety than on foot and at dramatically increased speeds. Ski descents can enable you to cover distances at the conclusion of your climb which would be unthinkable to the summer mountaineer. Mid-winter travel in the mountains often makes routes possible which in the summer are a jungle of thorn bushes, or a vast and painful talus slope or loose scree chute. In winter one can glide over all of this blissfully unaware of anything but the smooth snow which covers it.

Another point about mountains in the winter – you usually have them to yourself. In the summer half a dozen parties clambering simultaneously on to a summit can destroy the experience for me. In winter they are gone and peace returns.

Ski mountaineering is a dangerous sport and as such deserves immense respect. Knowledge and experience are the key to its safety. In Chapters Eight and Nine, I have brushed the surface of this aspect of skiing. Anyone contemplating mountain skiing should start by joining an experienced party.

Boots and bindings are also a problem. The light pin bindings and athletic shoe type boot do not offer sufficient control in soft snow. The force that can be transmitted to the ski through the three small pins in the bottom of the boot simply is insufficient. Cable bindings which enable the entire foot to apply leverage to the toe iron and thence to the ski are required. Unfortunately most of the boots have soles which are so flexible that they will not resist the compression produced by a cable around the heel. Also, the heels of most so called "touring" boots on the market are often so small that no cable will fit them. In an effort to make the equipment weightless the designers have neglected the requirement for torsional stiffness. Total flexibility fore and aft *is* a requirement for all cross-country skiing, but lateral stiffness or rigidity is still needed for directional control in deep snow.

Figure 1.15 Using the mountaineer's aids: rope, ice axe, and crampons, the mountain skier can climb to the heights from which exciting downhill runs are possible.

Figure 1.14 Skis enable the mountain visitor to travel distances which would seem incredible to the summertime hiker. (Mt. Cayley by Paul Starr).

Equipment required for ski mountaineering varies considerably. Most people use alpine equipment modified in such a way as to make walking and climbing possible. Climbing requires either the use of non-slip "skins" stretched over the bottom of one's ski or carrying the skis on one's shoulder, a most awkward activity. I am a strong advocate for use of normal deep snow touring equipment in the high mountains but am quick to point out that when icy or wind-packed conditions exist descents are far more difficult. To me these are small disadvantages since the pleasure of touring with the lighter equipment is so much greater.

There is a strong prejudice against the use of touring equipment in the high mountains on the part of the oldtime Swiss and Austrian guide fraternity. The reader should be forewarned that if he tries to bring his touring skis on established expeditions like helicopter skiing in the Bugaboos, or the Haute Route in the Alps, he will meet with substantial resistance. However, more and more high mountain ski tours and ski camps are being held in which touring skiers are welcome. With the coming of more general knowledge of downhill touring techniques I am sure more and more opportunities for skiing in the mountains will arise.

I practice mountain skiing on both types of equipment. I regularly visit Mount Washington's Tuckerman's Ravine every spring preferring my downhill skis for handling its precipitous slopes. On expeditions to Mount Washington's summit earlier in the season, when soft snow is more assured, I have used my touring skis.

While Chapter Three will describe some of the specialized alpine ski equipment available for mountain skiing, I do not propose to discuss alpine skiing techniques which are beyond the scope of this book.

19

ORIENTEERING ON SKIS

Orienteering on skis is a very old and popular sport in Scandinavia. The participants move from one checkpoint to another utilizing a map and compass and making decisions on the route as they go. The object is to complete a circuit course in as short a time as possible. Orienteering is a popular sport that can be done on foot, bicycle or skis. It is similar to an automobile rally in many respects in that it involves a keen sense of judgement of what is going to be the fastest route to get you from point A to point B and involves quick thinking and accurate use of map and compass.

Orienteering on skis is especially fun since the versatility of skis to cross any sort of terrain at speed is a great advantage. Equipment for orienteering on skis is virtually the same as for deep snow touring. (Relatively broad skis, often protected by a steel edge on the inside edge of each ski to assist in climbing and turning under icy conditions, are most desirable). The skis are rugged as often, in taking the shortest line between checkpoints, you will be travelling through brush and dense woods. Orienteering on skis is rapidly becoming popular here in North America also, and is a highly instructive way for young people to get to learn the skills of map and compass reading.

The essence of orienteering is developing good navigational judgement. I think it is essential grounding for anyone who wishes to become a proficient route finder in wilderness terrain.

Starting at timed intervals the participants visit the master map of the course and transfer the route to their own maps. Only the control points are marked, the route between them being entirely up to the competitor. An experienced orienteer will know that hills will eat up his energy and he will avoid them, at least at first. Taking a direct compass bearing on the desired control point is often less preferable to "aiming off" to a point near the control but which is more readily identifiable. This is called a "collecting feature" and greatly reduces the distance for which the orienteer must rely on his compass bearing alone in reaching the control. Hand holding a compass with any accuracy while running on skis is quite a trick. If the distance from your "collecting feature" is only a few hundred yards your chances of pulling it off are immeasureably improved. I remember once going out on a training run on foot with my cousin in Sweden, a champion orienteer, and running at break neck speed through a dense pine forest for what seemed like hours. All the time he was continually glancing at his compass and map while I simply struggled to keep up. Suddenly, when we emerged through the trees, immediately in front of us was a small viking "rune" stone not more than three feet high. This was the control point he had been aiming for! If we had been 10 yards to the left or right we would have missed it for sure.

It is this product of orienteering, a natural and instinctive ability to find your way around unknown country, which is so wonderful and more important than the competition itself. It's an experience well worth having.

To find out about orienteering meets in your area check your local ski association. Often team events are held in which families, schools, or clubs can field a team of 3 or 4 skiers.

An excellent reference for learning about orienteering and the use of map and compass is *Be Expert with Map and Compass* by B. Kjellstom.

DECIDING WHAT KIND OF SKIING IS FOR YOU

In order to reach a logical conclusion on what type of skiing to take up the beginner should evaluate the terrain he has access to. If it tends to be all flat and he likes to ski with groups of people, competition or plain trail skiing might easily be the most rational choice. A decision on whether to buy light touring skis or regular touring skis should be made on the basis of the availability of trails. If few other skiers and trails exist in his locality the new skier would probably be better off with standard touring skis so that he can more easily break out his own trail. If you are keen on learning to compete I would strongly advise putting off the purchase of racing skis until you have developed good technique. Premature use of super light skis will only delay development of good technique.

If you live in terrain which is very hilly or with large mountains you should certainly consider heavier touring equipment. This will enable you to gain maximum advantage from downhill technique in deep snow for which these conditions are ideal.

Figure 1.16 Orienteering often means taking the longer but faster route.

If the skier is a mountaineer or a very keen alpine or downhill skier he might well gravitate toward ski mountaineering *or* high country touring on alpine equipment converted for touring use. In this way it is possible to reach some spectacular downhill runs in the mountains without the expense of helicopters and in terrain where most other skiers do not venture.

Orienteering on skis is a very pleasureable way to get into the sport especially for young children, or teenagers because it adds another dimension of interest and challenge all of which contribute to its enjoyment.

Much of the confusion about the different types of cross-country skiing originates from the fact that skiing in general has progressed through its history from originally being purely a method of travelling on the level, to gradually descending hills for their own sake. Ski equipment, correspondingly, has developed over the years to make these activities easier. Gradually a separation has occurred between cross-country equipment and alpine or downhill equipment. The development of the rigid binding required for alpine techniques is a modern development, largely post-World War Two. Prior to this all ski equipment, even that intended for skiing down hills, had the necessary features for striding on the level and climbing. Many of us who learned to ski 20 to 40 years ago, started out on equipment

which was very similar to what I would consider ideal for deep snow touring today. Hence the tendency of many people to consider deep snow ski touring as an "old fashioned" concept.

Ultimately, you will only decide what kind of skiing really suits you by trying them all. In fact during the course of the season there are invariably occasions when one is more logical than another. Unfortunately, however, few of us are such enthusiasts that we are prepared to equip ourselves for more than one.

CHAPTER TWO
WHERE TO GO SKIING

GOOD INTRODUCTIONS TO SKIING FOR BEGINNERS

Since I am a great advocate of skiing across *any* country where there is snow it always bugs me when people ask "Where is a good place to go skiing?" Most of us always seem to need other people doing the same thing to feel comfortable. In many instances the companionship of others may enhance the activity, but in the case of cross-country skiing I believe skiing alone or in very small groups is far more pleasant! For one thing the snow is undisturbed by others, not to mention the absence of noise, crowds, traffic and the like.

I've always suggested to people who ask the question that they go to a country traditionally not thought of for skiing. Since there is such a vast variety of terrain that is suitable for cross-country skiing, all one needs is good snow. There are many areas in New England, Ontario and Québec far from any ski area where one can find good skiing and often very reasonable accommodation! For après ski you may have to be content with a local mill town pub or greasy spoon, but even this can have its attractions. Prices are usually far lower in these areas than near the big name ski developments.

The cross-country boom has breathed new life into the rural inn business. Many fine old country inns that over the years survived on summer golf, autumn foliage, and spring fishing, now have winter skiing to round out their year. Many have actually gone so far as to acquire equipment for rental, instructors, and developed groomed trails. Personally, I prefer the ones who have done nothing in particular except continue to supply good food and comfortable lodging.

However, I must temper my disdain for "organized" cross-country ski areas as I recognize full well that those trying skiing for the first time may well expect and prefer the many advantages of groomed trails, instruction, rental equipment, and most of all, others doing the same thing. You see, a few years ago most neophyte cross-country skiers were converted alpine skiers and already quite used to snow. Today more and more are completely new to winter and the outdoors. They used to be entirely "inside people" who confined their winter time outside activities to a week or two in the sun down south.

Figure 2.1 Organized lessons for cross-country skiers are probably useful for those who have never been on skis before, but are certainly not necessary.

Fortunately many fine ski touring centers have been developed to cater to these new skiers. It is an excellent idea to visit one before buying equipment, just to get an introduction. All of them have the advantage of being located in superb ski touring country and the chance of having a miserable time because you encountered poor conditions is correspondingly reduced. Just promise me that, having been to one or two, having equipped yourself with lessons, skis, and some enthusiasm for the sport, that you will venture forth to uncharted ski country and break your own trail! In doing so you will discover the vast prospects for this sport. If the skiing alone is not enough, try winter photography, game stalking, endurance treks, night skiing, winter camping . . . there are more and more possibilities . . . .

Figure 2.2 Discovery of man's summertime world deeply buried by the quiet winter snow makes one realize how dramatically our landscape changes through the months.

SPECTACULAR TERRAIN FOR SEASONED SKIERS

My next category of specific places to ski are areas containing spectacular terrain for ski touring. Again many of these are listed in the various directories. The ones which follow are generally not thought of as cross-country areas and as a result are sometimes not listed. These are places to go *after* you have acquired some technique, have your own equipment, and have become generally self-sufficient in the outdoors.

Alpine skiers have for several years now been lured to the undisturbed powder bowls in the Bugaboos, Cariboos and other mountains accessible via helicopter. This superb terrain is also available to the tour skier and mountain skier by foot for less cost. The best way to get there is in an organized party guided by experienced people who know the area very thoroughly. While I would

encourage any seasoned skier to develop the skills required to mount their own expedition, for most people this is impractical. Mountain ski touring guide services are developing rapidly at every area. One of the best ways to get into real mountain wilderness is by going to a ski mountaineering camp. Several are run each year by such organizations as

The Alpine Club of Canada
Box 1026,
Banff, Alberta T0L 0C0
and often space is available for non-members. Favorite areas are Skoki, Kokanee, Yoho, Assiniboine, Exemite/Tonquin, and Freshfields. The cost is nominal and the skiing guaranteed to be incredible. This is a good way to get more experience in the high mountains as you will meet and ski with expert mountain guides.

Most of the helicopter operators such as Hans Gmoser, of

Canadian Mountain Holidays,
P.O. Box 1660,
Banff, Alberta T0L 0C0
(403) 762-3381
are quite prejudiced against taking skiers using touring equipment to high elevations by aircraft. However, Hans runs ski tours on the ground into fabulous wilderness areas. I believe that gradually as more tour skiers demonstrate their ability to make steep descents in a variety of conditions, air lifts to high altitudes will become increasingly available. Write C.M.H. in Banff about their tours in The Little Yoho, Mummery Glacier, Mt. Assiniboine, Wapta Glacier and Northern Selkirks areas. Another ski tour operator everywhere from Mt. Assiniboine, to Skoki, to Yellowstone National Park is

Royal Gorge Ski Touring Inc.
P.O. Box 178,
Soda Springs, Colorado

Figure 2.3 Winter heightens contrasts, accentuates form . . . a photographer's dream.

WHERE TO SKI AS A COMPETITOR

Following is a list of major popular racing events which are internationally known. Each year dozens of new events are cropping up all around the country, so this list is by no means complete. Consult your local ski associations, ski clubs, and ski shops for calendars of local events. Cross-country races require dozens of people for trail marking, manning check points (to prevent people taking short cuts!) time keeping, and starting. Volunteers for these duties are *always* in demand. If you have a family member competing, this is one way you can get involved in some of the fun and excitement as well.

The Canadian Marathon is run the last weekend in February each year, over 90 miles (145 km) through country starting in the Laurentians, north of Montreal, and ending in the Gatineau Hills, outside Ottawa. This is a two day race with mass starts at 8:00 A.M. Saturday and Sunday. The course is divided into ten, approximately 10 mile (16 km) long sections and tour racers are not permitted to start a new section after 2:00 P.M. In 1976 entries were limited to the first 3000 competitors who applied. The $14.00 entry fee includes transportation service from finish points each day. Entry deadlines

are Dec. 15th. The course is well illustrated by detail maps and profiles of each section in a book that is provided for each registrant.
Write:
The Canadian Ski Marathon,
Box 315, Station A,
Ottawa K1N 8V3, Canada

The Washington's Birthday Ski Touring Race is run over an approximately 15 kilometer (9¼ mi.) course in the heart of Vermont's best touring country near the Putney School in Putney, Vermont. It is run on the Sunday closest to Washington's Birthday, February 22nd, and attracts many competitors.
Write:
The Washington's Birthday
Race Committee,
c/o The Putney School,
Putney, Vermont 05346

The Madonna Vasa covers 24 kilometers (15 mi.) between Madonna Mountain in Jeffersonville, Vermont, and Underhill Center. It is held the first Sunday in March, the same day as the Vasaloppet in Sweden.
Write:
Dr. John Bland,
Upper Valley Road,
Cambridge, Vermont 05444

The Stowe Derby is an annual 7 mile (11.3 km) event usually run in February.
Write:
Stowe Derby Race Committee,
c/o Stowe School,
Stowe, Vermont 05672

V-J-C Ski Touring Race is held outside Minneapolis in late February each year. Several hundred participants are normally expected.
Write:
North Star Ski Touring Club,
4231 Oakdale Avenue,
Minneapolis, Minnesota 55416

The John Craig Memorial Ski Touring Race is held early in April over an 18 mile (29 km) course, used by the pioneer ski mailman.
Write:
Oregon Nordic Club,
Bend,
Oregon 07701

The Estonian Open Ski Touring Race is a 20 kilometer (12.5 mi.) event usually held on the first weekend in March in country near the site of the Muskoka Loppett in Ontario. Come to this one and you will see the best racers.
Write:
The Estonian Ski Club
301 Riverside Road,
Oakville, Ontario

Top-of-the-World Championships is a complete Nordic X-try competition held in the first half of April in Inuvik, Northwest Territories. It is restricted to Divisional Teams by invitation only. Write to the Canadian Ski Association for complete information.

The American Birkebeiner is a 55 kilometer (34 mi.) annual event held on the 3rd weekend in February at Telemark in Wisconsin. It was started in 1975 to complement its Norwegian counterpart run between the villages of Lillehammer and Rena. Birkebeiner means "birch legs" and refers to the birch bark leggings worn by the Viking skiers who rescued the infant heir to the Norwegian throne, Hakon Hakonson during the 1206 Civil War. For more information contact:-
The American Birkebeiner,
Telemark Ski Area,
Cable, Wisconsin 54821
Tel: (715) 798-3811

The Engadin Marathon is a massive event staged since 1969 annually on the 2nd Sunday of March at St. Moritz/Pontresina. It is open to all skiers and in 1976 attracted 15,000! The distance is 42 kilometers (26 mi.) between the villages of Maloja and Zuoz - S. Chanf, losing approximately 100 meters of altitude along the way. The men's record is 1 hour 42 minutes. The geschmossel start must be really something! If you enter for 5 years in a row you gain enough seniority to start immediately behind the Elite Class racers. For more information write:
Engadin Skimarathon,
Maloja - Sils - Silvaplana,
CH - 7514 SILS/SEGL MARIA
Switzerland

The Colorado Gold Rush Ski Race is a family type event covering around 12 kilometers (8 mi.) near Breckenridge, Colorado, at 10,000 feet.
Write:
Chamber of Commerce,
Frisco, Colorado 80433

The Muskoka Loppet is a 30 kilometer (18½ mi.) event through beautiful forests in the Muskoka Lakes region in Ontario. It is run on the second Sunday in January and attracts several hundred entrants.
Write:
Muskoka Winter Association,
Box 1239,
Huntsville, Ontario, Canada

Jack Rabbit Family Ski Tour is an annual event run early in March over a 16 kilometer (10 mi.) course in Southern Ontario.
Write:
The Jack Rabbit Ski Club,
Attention: Neil MacDonald,
341 Dixon Park Cresent,
Mississauga, Ontario

SISU Races run on the first weekend in February at the Finnish Ski Club in Udora, Ontario, attract top quality racers for 5, 10, 15 and 30 kilometer (3-18½ mi.) events. Enjoy a sauna and Finnish cooking too!
Write:
SISU Ski Club,
c/o Mr. Markku Rojala,
2200 Avenue Road, Apt. 601,
Toronto 380, Ontario

Figure 2.4 The Muskoka Loppet – Mass Start.

Figure 2.5 Refueling stop at the Muskoka Loppet. (Such services are included in the entry fee.)

Figure 2.6 Even a double track cannot absorb the skiers near the start.

Figure 2.7 That delicious fatigue which comes at the end makes it all worthwhile.

SKIING ABROAD

A ski trip to Europe need not be for alpine skiing at all. Indeed, alpine purists all maintain that ski conditions are generally better in the American and Canadian West than abroad. However, the spectacular scenery and beautiful après ski food and the like, are strong attractions to going abroad. All of these are of course available to the tour skier as well. The high accessibility of the European peaks means that it is easy to cross-country ski in exciting terrain.

The Scandinavian countries are very popular for ski touring as it has been a traditional way of life there for so many years. Contact the national airlines for each country to get information on ski/flight/accommodation packages and good places to go.

Scandinavia
Cross-country touring in Norway and Sweden is generally developed for foreign tourists near the popular alpine ski centers. Tyin, Norefjell, Geilo, Voss in Norway have excellent facilities. The beautiful forests of Nordmarka just outside Oslo are beautiful. The annual Holmenkollen Nordic ski meet is held there on the 2nd weekend in March each year. Don't miss seeing the Ski Museum at Holmenkollen which is open year round.

In Sweden, Falun is the principal skiing center, but ski touring abounds everywhere. The Vasaloppet is held on the first Sunday in March each year, so a single trip taking it *and* Holmenkollen is feasible.

Europe
If you dream of skiing from village to village on skis, sampling the accommodation on the way, Europe is the place to go. Many of the classic alpine runs such as the "Parsenn", an uninterrupted 15

Figure 2.8 The incredible Engadin Ski Marathon.

mile trail from Davos to Klosters can easily be done on touring equipment early in the season when there is plenty of powder snow along the way. When you arrive in Klosters after the 3 or 4 hour (comfortable) trip, stop in at a local "Stubli" for a warm drink and then take the train back to Davos.

Off-the-trail tours in Europe are best done with a guide, as it is easy to wander into avalanche country even within a stone's throw of the established ski runs. The possibilities for exciting tours is endless and there are always friendly (and inexpensive) guides to help you. Often it will be a good idea to arrange a short helicopter flight to your starting point. To make these arrangements and locate a guide, plan to arrive a day or two early at your destination before leaving on a trek. High mountain huts often make it possible to stay for many days high in the mountains with a minimum of gear.

The most sensational of all high tours in Europe is the so called "Haute Route" or high route between Saas Fee in the Swiss Valais and Chamonix in France. Customarily this is a spring tour done on alpine skis modified for touring or ski mountaineering (mid April to mid May is normal). An earlier trip can be arranged and barring weather problems can give spectacular skiing on lighter equipment. There are two routes, The Southern, (East to West from Saas Fee to Chamonix) or the Northern (in the opposite direction). On the Southern route you take the cable car from Courmayeur, Italy to Pointe Helbrunner, ski down the Vallée Blanche across the Mer de Glace and then take the train into Chamonix. The Northern route is generally considered more difficult. The whole trip takes 5 to 7 days but one must allow an additional 3 to 4 days for bad weather. Mountain skis, climbing skins, and bindings offering the possibility of stem turns are required for the trip. Nights are spent in Swiss Alpine Club huts staffed with keepers who do the cooking. It is possible to ski down into villages at night to the luxury of hotels if you wish. Arranging transport back to your party in the morning, while possible, can sometimes be awkward however.

SKIING TERRAIN AND WEATHER

As you acquire knowledge of local places to ski you will discover that there are invariably good places to go, regardless of weather conditions. I suggest looking for the following terrain under the following conditions:

Cold Temperatures, No Wind, New Snow
Ideal conditions for anywhere, but perfect for the big, open slopes which, all too often, are windblown. Perfect, too, for a summit climb.

Cold Temperatures, New Snow, but Windy
Seek out coniferous forests, avoid open terrain.

Cold Temperatures, Old Snow, but Windy
Tough conditions, but still good skiing will exist in a coniferous forest where the trees are well spaced. A good day for an athletic 'bushwack'' through forested terrain.

Cold Temperatures, Old Snow, but Calm
Look for the open slopes protected from high winds where the snow will still be soft. Try the "edge" of pastures, near the trees or a stone wall. Ideal conditions, too, for skiing in an open hardwood forest or a Vermont "sugar bush".

Late Winter, Bare Ground at Home, Old Crusty Snow in the Woods
Search out forests and ravines where the snow will remain. Often the drift line on the lee of stone walls in open fields will still provide good skiing in the sun. Look into old gravel pits and other steep terrain protected from the sun for some exciting telemarks. A great day for a picnic with plenty of dry places to sit and sunbathe!

Warm Temperatures, Old Crusty Snow
Search for the sun and shelter from wind. The snow will soften quickly with "use" providing for good telemarks. On a cooler day these are very fast conditions for a good, *long* tour.

Warm Temperatures, New Wet Snow
Whether windy or calm these conditions require either steep open terrain to permit good runs, or heavily forested terrain where the snow will still be soft. Do not try a long trip as the going can be very tiring. A great day for building a "jump" with children and skiing in a single area. Once a slope has been "broken out", telemarking will be easy.

Figure 2.9 Cold crisp snow; no wind; a perfect day to look for untouched slopes.

Figure 2.10 The hardwood forest protects the snow, keeping conditions perfect long after the open slopes are windpacked.

OFF-SEASON SKIING

If you're really keen there is good skiing to be had in the southern hemisphere during our summer season. Ski touring in *South America* is virtually non-existent, but I am sure many good possibilities are there for the adventurous. Most skiing is strictly alpine, introduced by Europeans 20 to 30 years ago. Boniloche in Argentina and Portillo in Chile are the principal areas.

Down under, in Australia, cross-country skiing has really taken hold. The great dividing range which runs from Queensland south through New South Wales to Victoria is 2500 miles long and contains snowfields larger than all of Switzerland's. July and August are the peak months for skiing and the "Snowy Mountains" between Melbourne and Canberra are the principal ski zone.

Mount Kosciusko at 7300 feet is the highest point of land, but the well weathered and eroded, rolling terrain of the Snowy Mountains makes ideal touring terrain.

Principal ski "areas" are Thredbo, Perisher, and Smiggin Holes in New South Wales, and Mt. Buller and Falls Creek in Victoria. These areas are 300 miles or more from Sydney and Melbourne. For information on touring and the hut system in Kosciusko National Park write:

Paddy Pallin Pty. Ltd.,
69 Liverpool Street,
Sydney, NSW.

Powder snow is rare in Australia, but the open, high terrain and the sight of green snow gum eucalypti trees filled with parrots arising from the snow make it an extraordinary place to ski.

Figure 2.11 When it snows, ski downtown.

NIGHT TOURING

Cross-country skiing at night can be a delightful way to work off a big evening meal! Moonlight is ample illumination in open country, but in heavy woods you will need a headlamp. These are available in any mountaineering equipment supply store for $10 to $20. The best type consists of a small battery cannister which you can wear inside your parka, so that the batteries stay warm, and a very light headlamp on a stretch band. (The "Justrite" is a popular model. It boasts a 1500 foot beam from 4 - "D" batteries, weighs 8 oz. without batteries and cost $10.25).

In Sweden many of the touring trails around Stockholm are actually lit at night. Personally, I think I prefer moonlight.

Figure 2.12 The Justrite Headlamp. This inexpensive ($10) device projects a 1500' beam and makes nighttime touring possible when there is no moon. Keep the battery pack inside your pocket where it will stay warm.

Figure 2.13 Children like the pace of cross-country skiing; there is no waiting; there is always something to do, places to explore.

Skiing with children younger than three is very easy as well. A newborn baby can snuggle comfortably against its mother's chest and be very secure from the effects of any fall. A simple child carrier can be obtained (see the Gerry "cuddler", about $8.50) to hold the child securely. After 9 and 12 months most babies have grown to the point where a back carrier is required. When the child is still very light he or she may face backwards slouched in the seat. When they get to be about 2 years they are so heavy that they must face forward. (The Gerry Kiddie Pack at about $18 is a good one). My son always held his hands over my eyes as we skied together!

Cross-country touring away from a trail makes it easier to combine skiers with a variety of abilities. This is true because the better ones can take longer routes, or more runs on any given hill. Our tours seem to be from one telemark slope to another. Also, the stronger skiers can break trail and the younger ones enjoy faster and easier going in broken snow.

CHILDREN AND SKIING

I have found cross-country skiing to be very well received by children. Initially they like it because as rank beginners they can go out and do it with adults. In downhill skiing they are confined to the kiddie slope for the first couple of years and suffer all the discomfort of heavy equipment, getting cold, trouble with handling the lift, etc. As cross-country skiers they have very few problems by comparison. One prime reason is that the experience need not last more than a few hours, while a downhill outing generally lasts all day. We often leave the house at a leisurely ten or eleven A.M. and are home for a late lunch around two P.M. Even with lunch on the trail we are always home, well exercised and refreshed, long before the downhill skiers have escaped their traffic jams. I have found it quite practical to put three-year-olds on skis and have been amazed at how well they can keep up with a group if they are skiing in a good track to guide their skis. Once about 6 or 8 they will sometimes get bored, although I've found various games such as "Fox and Geese" on a field or lake can amuse them. One thing I've often done when conditions are poor is to build a small ski jump. Scraping a bit of snow together to form a take-off requires only moments. Jumps of 20 feet or 30 feet are quite easily achieved even by children. If conditions are firm this can be quite hard on light cross-country skis, but it is a great confidence builder for any child. They will quickly learn the telemark position to prevent falls on landing.

Figure 2.14 The nemesis of the cross-country skier. The noisy, smelly snowmobile represents the antithesis of what skiing is all about. No more directly contradictory objectives could be held by these two groups who, unfortunately, must use the same environment.

SNOWMOBILES AND CROSS-COUNTRY SKIING

The snowmobiling craze fortunately, is tapering off as people recognize the environmental impact of these infernal machines. Advertised without sound on television they appear to be a miraculous machine. Indeed, they have at least wrenched hundreds of thousands of folks away from the television set into the outdoors.

Their incompatibility with cross-country skiing arises first from their extreme noise which is the very antithesis of what skiing is all about. A second problem is that they leave a firm, smooth track through the snow which is most awkward to ski in. On a steeply descending trail this track can make turning virtually impossible driving the skier off into the woods. Successive machines continually consolidate even soft snow until it is hard and unforgiving ice.

It is wise, therefore, to seek out areas to ski where snowmobiles are prohibited. Failing this, I find that if I stay in the dense woods, and on relatively steep slopes, I seldom run into them.

My fury over snowmobiles was raised to a high pitch when, during the Canadian Ski Marathon, one pulled onto the trail in front of me, refusing to let me pass, pouring noxious fumes into my face!

As a cross-country skier, one should campaign against the proliferation of snowmobiles at every opportunity.

To assist those interested in all aspects of cross-country skiing in finding good places to go skiing, I am listing below some sources for more information. It is impossible to mention every place and undoubtedly my list is very incomplete. I strongly recommend that you develop an information file and keep it current. By writing places that advertise in ski magazines you will gradually accumulate a large number of alternatives. To get your file started I offer the following:

For *new skiers seeking equipment rental, instruction, and an introduction to trail skiing.*

East

Ski New England
Box 800
Campton, New Hampshire 03223

Viking Ski Touring Centre
Little Pond Road,
Londonderry, Vermont 05148
(802) 824-3933

Trapp Family Lodge
Stowe, Vermont 05672
(802) 253-8511

Sugarbush Inn
Warren, Vermont 05674
(802) 583-2605

Blueberry Hill Skiing Center
Goshen, Vermont 05733
(802) 247-6735

Woodstock Ski Touring Center
Woodstock, Vermont 05091
(802) 457-2112

Sunshine Ski Touring Center
Box 18
Troy, Vermont 05868

Lake Placid Club
Lake Placid, New York 12946
(518) 523-3361

EMS Ski Touring Center
Intervale, New Hampshire 03845
(603) 356-5606

Sunday River Ski Touring Center
Bethel, Maine 04217
(207) 824-2410

Mohawk Mountain Ski Area
West Cornwall, Connecticut 06796
(203) 672-6100

Blackberry River Inn Ski Center
Rt. 44
Norfolk, Connecticut 06058
(203) 542-5100

Craigmeur Ski Area
Greenpond Road
Newfoundland, New Jersey 07435
(201) 679-4501

Hidden Valley Ski Area
RD #6
Somerset, Pennsylvania 15501
(814) 445-6014

L'Esterel
Box 38
Ville d'Esterel, Quebec J0T 1E0
(514) 228-2571

Chateau Montebello
Montebello, Quebec
(819) 423-6341

Horseshoe Valley Resort
Box 607
Barrie, Ontario
(705) 835-2014

Grey Rocks Inn
Box 1000
St. Jovite, Quebec
(819) 425-2771

* Appalachian Mountain Club
Pinkham Notch Camp
Gorham, New Hampshire 03581
(603) 466-3994

Cannon Mountain
Franconia, New Hampshire 03580
(603) 823-5563

* Ward Pound Reservation
Westchester County Parks &
Recreation Department
White Plains, New York 10601
(914) SU3-3493

* Jefferson National Forest
c/o Appalachian Outfitters
Rt. 3, Box 7A
Salem, Virginia 24153
(603) 389-1056

* Monongahela National Forest
Contact:
District Ranger US Forest Service
Petersburg, West Virginia 26847
(304) 275-7111

Midwest

Birchwood Farm Lodge
Harbor Springs, Michigan 49740
(616) 526-2151

Ken-Mar on the Hill
Box 679
Gaylor, Michigan 49735
(517) 732-4950

The Farm
Brantwood, Wisconsin 54513
(715) 564-2558

Telemark Ski Area
Cable, Wisconsin 54821
(715) 798-3811

West

Club Innisfree
8020 N. Lake Blvd.
King's Beach, California 95719
(916) 546-4242

Kirkwood Ski Touring Center
Box 77
Kirkwood, California 95646
(209) 258-8864

Squaw Valley Nordic Ski Center
Box 2288
Olympic Valley, California 95730
(916) 583-4316

Scandinavian Lodge
Box 5040
Steamboat Village, Colorado 80499

Vail Ski Touring Center
Box 819
Vail, Colorado 81657
(303) 476-3116

Yosemite National Park
California 94389
(209) 372-4611

Rocky Mountain Ski Tours
P.O. Box 413
Estes Park, Colorado 80517
(303) 586-2114

Craters of the Moon
National Monument
P.O. Box 29
Arco, Idaho 83213
(203) 527-3257

* Mt. Hood
Contact:
Mazamas Mountaineering Club
909 N.W. 19th Street
Portland, Oregon 97209
(503) 227-2345

* Mt. Ranier
Contact:
Supt. Mt. Ranier National Park
Longmire, Washington 98397
(206) 569-2211

* North Cascade Range
Contact:
Northwest Alpine Guide Service
1628 Ninth Street
Scattle, Washington 98101
(206) 622-6074

* Yellowstone Park
Contact: Parklands Expeditions
Box 371
Jackson Hole, Wyoming 83001
(307) 733-3379

Banff National Park
Contact: Banff-Lake Louise
Chamber of Commerce
Box 1298
Banff, Alberta T0L 0C0
(403) 762-3777

Jasper Park/Marmot Basin
Contact:
Jasper Chamber of Commerce
Box 98
Jasper, Alberta T0E 1E0
(403) 852-3858

National Tourist Offices

The Austrian National
Tourist Offices,
545 Fifth Avenue,
New York City, New York 10017
(212) 697-0651

Scandinavian Tourist Bureau,
75 Rockefeller Plaza,
N.Y. N.Y. 10016
(212) 582-2802

Airlines

SAS
638 Fifth Avenue,
N.Y. N.Y. 10020
(212) 977-2620

Swissair,
608 Fifth Avenue,
N.Y. N.Y. 10020
(212) 995-8400

SAS, Ski Desk,
800 Dorchester Blvd. W.,
Suite 530
Montreal, Quebec
(514) 861-8317

Swissair
2 Carlton Street,
Toronto, Ontario
(416) 364-3361

Finnair,
8 King Street East,
Toronto, Ontario
(416) 362-1511

Many comprehensive listings of such resorts are published by ski magazines each year. These will contain a short description of each place and make it much easier to narrow down your choice. One of the best directories is *The Ski Touring Guide* published by the Ski Touring Council Inc., Troy, Vermont 05868.

* *These locations offer the experienced skier with his own equipment ample opportunity for off-the-trail skiing in deep snow*

Figure 2.15 Taking off on your own into winter country – a great feeling.

CHAPTER THREE
EQUIPMENT FOR CROSS-COUNTRY SKIING

Figure 3.1 Equipment merchandising can baffle the beginning skier.

EQUIPMENT FOR CROSS-COUNTRY SKIING

I hope before you set out to buy any equipment you have reached some conclusions on what type of skiing you wish to do. As for any sport, equipment for cross-country skiing is rather specific. Except for the racer who may have four different pairs of skis for four different sorts of race courses, most cross-country skiers must settle for a single pair of skis. Inevitably, you must compromise at times. Your deep snow touring skis won't be ideal for that one race a year you decide to run in. Assess your skiing habits and intentions carefully and develop your own specifications for your equipment before you even visit a shop.

Once you do start to shop beware of a few problems. First, don't automatically trust the sales person for advice. Cross-country has grown incredibly rapidly and most people selling the equipment have as little actual experience using it as you do. Secondly, choose your specific items carefully making sure they are in perfect condition. Thirdly, beware of autumn specials on last year's equipment, unless you are pretty sure it has been stored properly. Fourthly, be extremely critical of ski shop binding installations. Make sure the boots are directly aligned with the ski and insist on an adjustment if they are not. Check serial numbers to insure the skis are the ones you selected. Note where the binding has been installed. And finally, be very cautious of package deals since often they are a way for a retailer to unload items which aren't selling for some good reason.

Equipment for cross-country skiing is modest in cost and its performance must be excellent if you are to enjoy the sport. So why skimp on any of it? Buy good quality, once you know what you want.

If you're unsure, rent equipment once or twice. Experiment with waxing, and with no-wax skis. Discover your own preferences for yourself.

ALL ABOUT BOOTS

Boots are unquestionably the most important piece of equipment which the skier uses in that they are closest to his body and, in fact, form the only physical connection between it and his skis. They must fit extremely well and offer the degree of support that is required for the type of skiing he is carrying on. To date no manufacturer has found a material more satisfactory than leather for the boot uppers. The vinyls used on many of the cheaper boots do not breathe to the extent that leather does, and consequently, perspiration within the boot can cause the feet to get wet, and then cold, far sooner than with a leather boot. On the other hand, vinyl boots dry out much faster and require virtually no maintenance. These have to be secondary considerations after comfort, although I think vinyl boots are perfectly OK for youngsters and adults who will ski only a few hours at a time.

Figure 3.2 The Author's boots. (From left to right) racing boots, light touring boots suitable for a pin binding, touring boots for a cable binding, ski mountaineering boots with a flexible Vibram sole.

Figure 3.3 When fitting the boot insure that there is a finger's breadth of space in front of your toes.

Cross-country boots range from the inexpensive light touring or racing models in vinyl (about $20), to ski mountaineering types ($90). Good general touring models are quite expensive at $45 to $70, or more. All skiers should select their boots after having selected their bindings as both of these pieces of equipment must be totally compatible. It is essential that the shape and characteristics of the sole match the requirements of the binding. Pin bindings demand reinforced sockets for pins. Some boots with a crêpe type sole advertise that they don't need sockets – don't believe them. All pin bindings now are manufactured around the so called "Nordic Norm" sole profile so there is little difficulty in that regard. Be careful that your binding is the appropriate model for your boot size.

If you have elected to use a cable binding you must select a boot with a grooved heel. Many touring boots have tiny heels with a small groove around them. These are *not* appropriate for cable bindings. It is essential that the heel be comparable in size to that on a street shoe if it is to hold the cable in place. Some cable bindings, such as the Norwegian "Tempo", employ a rigid heel piece which must be contoured to fit the heel perfectly if it is to stay on. It also requires a broader groove in the heel, as does the coil spring type of cable. Conventional cables with a rubber sleeve around them will work on any kind of groove.

With a cable binding the sole of the boot must be stiff enough so that it does not collapse when bent at an acute angle and squeezed at the heel. The sole ideally should be of leather but this is virtually impossible to find these days as every manufacturer has converted to molded composition soles. If the boot sole collapses in this way you will find that your cable bindings constantly come off. Some boots have a steel or wooden fibreglass shank imbedded in their sole to allow bending only in one place. I am not convinced however that any contemporary boot on the North American market has really been designed with the requirements of the cable binding in mind.

Actually, all cross-country boots need a torsionally rigid sole. If you grasp the heel and toe and wring the boot like a dish rag, the more resistance the better the boot is. It is beyond me why so many manufacturers have narrowed their soles to the point where they have virtually no torsional rigidity.

Figure 3.4 The sole of the boot to be used in a cable binding must be torsionally rigid.

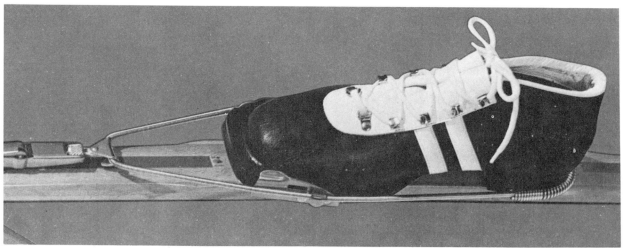

The cut of the boot upper is of relatively little consequence for tour skiers although I would recommend an above-the-ankle type for anyone who intends to do a lot of deep snow touring. For light touring it really does not matter. Low boots with an elasticized cuff are often better at keeping the snow out than higher ones without cuffs. I always wear anklets or gaiters, anyway, so this is not a consideration. The higher cut boots do offer more support. If you are going to do mountain skiing you should definitely go to a higher cut boot with a greater support. If you are serious about high country touring you will want to purchase ski mountaineering boots which have cleated "Vibram" soles making them suitable for walking or cramponing as well. Often you may wish to kick steps or crampon up a steep snow field or climb along a rocky wind swept ridge carrying your skis. Conventional touring boots would be very slippery for this. Figure 3.2 illustrates the range of boots from the lightest racing shoe to ski mountaineering boots.

When trying on your boots make sure that you have at least a finger's breadth of space in front of your toes. Bend forward on your knees with the boots laced properly and bent as if in a binding, and insure that your toes are not pinched. The heels should fit snugly and not tend to ride up and down as you move your foot. Don't buy oversized boots for children to grow into since this will only result in blisters.

In the past, cross-country boots seldom appeared at annual ski swaps because there were so few around. Today, this is changing and it is quite easy to keep children outfitted in used boots each year.

Figure 3.5 Light touring boots designed for pin binding. Note toe protector with "notches" at holes.

Adults looking for good quality touring boots have a much harder time. Local ski shops seldom have a decent stock. Buying boots by mail (see Sources for Equipment) is not an impractical idea at all. Simply make a tracing of your foot with normal ski socks on. Hold the pencil vertically and in firm contact with your foot all the way round.

Most mail order houses will hit the right size on the first try. If not, it is not hard to return them for a size larger or smaller. The touring boots that I use all the time I bought by mail from Gresvig in Oslo 15 years ago. They came to me within 10 days of placing my order and fitted perfectly! The total cost was $12!

Insulation in a light touring or racing boot is definitely not necessary. Avoid fleece linings which only get wet. In normal skiing your feet should stay quite comfortable just from moving around. Composition soles however are quite poor insulators so if you stand around much your feet will get cold. Inner soles may be an answer. Heavier touring boots and ski mountaineering boots should be lined to improve warmth, especially if you intend to do any winter camping in them.

Figure 3.6 Alpine Ski Boots for ski mountaineering. These are much heavier boots without the flexible sole required for Nordic technique. (Size 9 weighs 7 lbs. 3 oz.) On the left, the plastic support cover is in place; on the right, it is removed. Note the steep angled heel groove adaptable only to Alpine type bindings.

Top racing boots available in North America are the Adidas "Lahti" (leather) or "Suomi" (nylon) models (which must be used with the Adidas binding that comes with the boot); Caber "competition", Fauker "Thoma", Jette "competition", Perssons "model 475", Skilom "Lillehammer", Trak "competition", or Tiger "X-C".

Top quality *light touring boots* available in North America include: Trysil Knut "model 229", Tyrol "strom", Kikut "908", Skilom "Oslo-2067", Norge "299U", Jette #666, Haugen "toast", Fels "#913", Kikut "1800", Fabiano "Nicole", or Edsbyn "#8109".

Heavier Touring boots available in North America of excellent quality and suitable for cable bindings would include: the Alfa "1001", Fabiano "Edwards", Jette "621", Nørrøna Model 1221, or SILVA "215".

The area of *Ski Mountaineering boots* is where the selection really shortens – only Nørrøna model 1030, and Kikut model 813 are available that I know of. Both have "Vibram" soles and are of excellent quality.

An excellent *Alpine* type Ski Mountaineering boot is the "Haute Route" by Hanwag. Conventional mountaineering boots can be modified for alpine skiing use only by the addition of "spoilers" popular in Europe. These are available from Sporthaus Schuster in Munich.

Care and Maintenance of Boots
Everyone knows, I am sure, about the fundamentals: never dry your boots by the fire (that includes camp fires) or a warm air radiator. Use merely a warm/dry place instead. Blocking of cross-country boots is not very important since the sole should remain flexible in any event. The boot will dry out better with nothing in it anyway. First, clean the boots with saddle soap and warm water using a brush and then allow to dry thoroughly.

Figure 3.7 Nørrona Mountain Touring Boots. Weighing less than 4 lb. these are ideal high country ski boots having a flexible Vibram sole and heel grooved for regular Touring bindings.

Leather is made to be worn by the animal it came from. Once made into boots it must be constantly conditioned by the addition of special compounds to waterproof and condition the leather. The kind of compound to use depends on the method of tanning that was used in making your boot leather. Boot leather is either *chrome* tanned or *oil* tanned. Chrome tanning, commonly used for hiking boots, involves removing all natural oils and substituting chromium salts which gives the boot a hard dry looking surface. Oil tanning involves replacement of natural oils with vegetable products giving a much softer leather which looks moister and shinier.

Figure 3.7a Sno-Seal: an excellent silicone/wax preservative.

To waterproof and condition your boots just apply some liquid silicone allowing it to soak in around the sole welting. Chrome tanned boots require waxes preferably mixed with silicone as in "Sno-Seal". Oil tanned boots should have oil based conditioners used such as "Mink oil". Rub the conditioner into the boot while warm, thoroughly kneading it in with your fingers. Wipe off excess and allow to dry briefly before going skiing.

If in doubt about the tanning process used on your boots use the wax and silicone process. Never use oil based conditioners on chrome tanned leather as it can ruin it. Thorough scrubbing and cleaning of leather boots periodically followed by waterproofing will greatly increase their life. Always leave your boots well preserved between seasons and store in a cool dry place where they will not become moldy.

Properly cared for, cross-country boots of all types should last for many seasons. Mine are 15 years old and I expect them to last at least 15 more years!

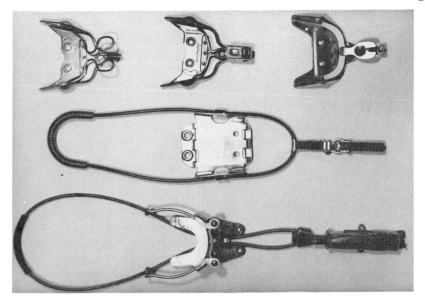

Figure 3.9 Typical pin binding with one piece "Nordic Norm" toe piece.

Figure 3.8 Bindings for cross-country skiing. Types range from lightweight pin or toe bindings to Silvretta Cable Binding for ski mountaineering.

ALL ABOUT BINDINGS

Bindings must be selected at the same time as the boot for the two must be 100% compatible. Nothing is more aggravating than a binding which persists in coming off or one which fails to give the required control. Points to keep in mind are:
(1) Does the toe iron fit the sole profile? Is it Nordic Norm and if so is it the size Nordic Norm required for your boot size?
(2) Is the design compatible with the kind of skiing you anticipate doing? Presumably you will have committed yourself in one direction or another in selecting your boots.
(3) Are the mounting screw spacings appropriate for the width of ski you will be using? Often they are not, with outer screws either spaced so far apart that they don't even go into the wood, or so close to the edge that tightening the screws will cause the ski to split. I once saw a ski shop offering a "cross-country package" where this was the case. I asked the owner why he supplied that binding with that ski and he said "You don't really need those outside holes anyway, we simply leave those screws out"!

In fact the outermost screws absorb the most force of all and should always be used. Pin bindings to be used with light touring or racing boots generally are attached with three screws. Drilling of the ski must be extremely precise as there is no adjustment.

One added complication is that when you mark the holes you can't have the boots in the binding since they would cover the holes. There is, therefore, no way of being absolutely certain that the heel of the boot will be dead centered on the ski, as it should be, once the binding is screwed on. Unfortunately having the ski shop mount your bindings is no guarantee that the job will be done correctly. However I would not recommend that you do it yourself unless you've had some experience. Screw holes for ski bindings should always be drilled with a tapered drill precisely related to the screw size to insure a tight fit. I always scrape some ski wax on the screw before inserting it to lessen the hazard of cracking or splitting, and allowing greater torquing of the screws.

Cross-country bindings are mounted in a position so that the joint between the boot upper and the sole falls at the balance point of the ski. This means that the ball of the foot falls several inches behind the balance point. When the ski is picked up vertically the tip will droop immediately.

Pin Bindings for racing and light touring are made by innumerable manufacturers with 2 pins and 3 pins, clamping bails to hold the boot in and fastened by simply pushing with a ski pole (called step-in-step-out feature), and come in all colours and weights. Rottefella is the oldest manufacturer with models starting as low as $6. I find the wire type bails very flimsy, preferring instead the spring steel type.

Skilom makes a pin binding out of Delrin plastic but I am unsure what its advantages might be.

An interesting variation on the pin binding is the "longstep" binding made in Switzerland. It incorporates a pin hinge between the portion clamped to the boot and the portion screwed to the ski. It is expensive ($25) but has several advantages: the length of the stride is supposedly increased, feet stay warmer and more comfortable, and it is very easy to mount since the boot can be placed in the binding and perfectly aligned before holes are marked and drilled (see Figure 3-10).

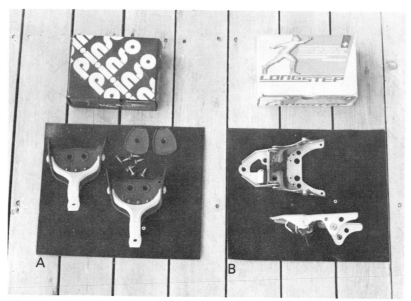

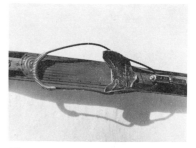

Figure 3.11 The Author's own Kandahar Cable Binding made by Gresvig. This one piece "Nordic Norm" toe assembly is anodized aluminum and extremely light.

Figure 3.10 (A) All Plastic Pin Binding by Pinso. (B) Swiss made Longstep Binding.

All pin bindings require a heel pad or "pop up" to prevent snow from building up under the foot and to protect the ski from wear. The best kind have serrated metal teeth so they can be used to scrape the snow from your boots when putting on the skis.

Cable Bindings for deep snow touring fall into 3 categories: those with shortening clamps at the heel such as the Norwegian "Tempo", those with a front throw for tightening such as the Gresvig "Kandahar", and ski mountaineering models which allow for heel hold down for alpine technique and which have safety release features such as the "Silvretta" or Ramy Securus. Cost range from $12 to $45.

Finding cable bindings of good quality is not easy. Since most incorporate an adjustable toe iron it is not absolutely essential that they be purchased with the boots. I prefer models with front throws finding them somewhat easier to put on than the heel clamp type. Ideally the front throw should be of the reverse type which you pull towards you as this lessens the danger of them coming undone due to skiing in crusty snow or hitting a branch in the woods.

I've never found much need for a release feature on a touring binding such as provided by the Silvretta or Ramy Securus. But then, I've never attempted to ski alpine technique on touring skis. These bindings are designed for use on alpine skis with a rigid boot only. One combination I did try briefly some years ago was one using a long thong with a touring cable binding. The thong provided substantial support for edge control and could be totally removed for touring, leaving only two small rings. Today I'm sure no one even sells long thongs any more!

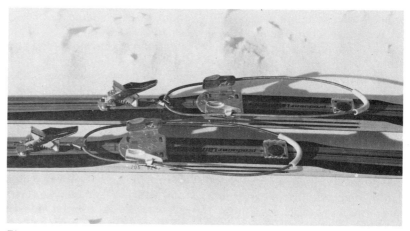

Figure 3.12 Sekur Cable Bindings made in Finland. These have adjustable toe plates and with their flexible cables can fit a wide variety of boots.

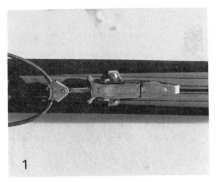 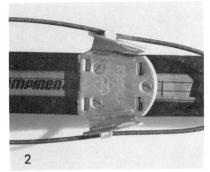 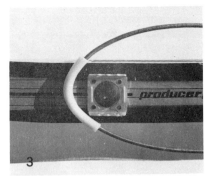

Figure 3.13 The elements of a Cable Binding: 1 Front Throw. (This one tends to open unexpectedly in deep snow where there is brush.); 2 Toe Plate-adjustable; 3 Heel Plate and "Pop-up".

ALL ABOUT SKIS

Cross-country ski types are categorized as racing, light touring (tur-langren), touring (Tur), and mountain touring (Fjellski). The widths of the skis vary from 35 to 45 mm measured at the "shovel" (or its broadest part immediately behind the tip) for racing skis, 40 to 50 mm for light touring, 45 to 60 mm for touring, and 65 to 75 mm or more for mountain touring. Weights for a pair 205 cm long vary from 2 lbs 12 oz (1.24 kg) for Kneissel racing skis to 6 lbs 8 oz (2.74 kg) for Trysil-Knut Fjell or mountain skis. This compares with over 12 lbs (5.4 kg) for a pair of comparable length alpine skis. Costs range from as little as $40 for light touring models in wood to $160 or more for special metal and plastic mountain skis. Materials for skis vary from laminated wood to all fibreglass with innumerable combinations in between.

Also available are numerous waxless or no-wax skis which employ mechanical deformations on the ski sole to prevent backslip. These are either "negative" in the form of diamonds, steps, or scoops, machined from or molded into the plastic bottom, (see Figure 3-20) or "positive" in the form of "fish scales" also molded into the bottom but projecting in varying degrees to

correspond to the primary gliding and kicking portions of the ski. Also in this category are skis with mohair strips fastened to the bottom principally where the ski is loaded during the kick phase.

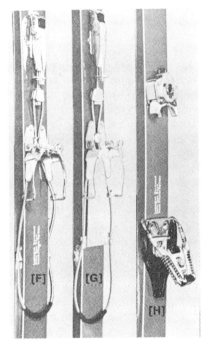

Figure 3.14 Bindings for ski mountaineering. All of these bindings require the use of Alpine Boots (see Figure 3-7). The "Silvretta" (G) is perhaps the most popular.

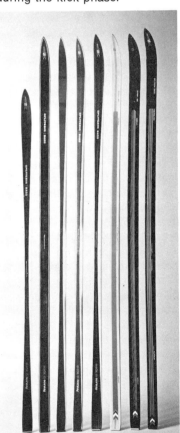

Figure 3.15 Skis for a range of cross-country skiing. Widths vary from 38mm Racing Models to 75mm Mountain Touring types.

43

The recent surge in cross-country skiing has exploded the market for skis so dramatically that the oldtime suppliers could not possibly supply it. The result is that alpine ski manufacturers have jumped in to capitalize on this new market. They've adapted their production techniques for alpine skis to produce cross-country skis with a minimum of changes. Since the alpine skis are traditionally a much higher priced product it became necessary to promote receptiveness for price increases among cross-country buyers. In many cases the small older manufacturers were bought-out or simply went out of business in the face of so much new competition. A few such as Bonna, joined the fibreglass revolution. All skis have soared in price as a consequence. Those still making wood skis complain about the high cost of labour required to finish them. Many wood skis used to be hand-sanded and shaped to reduce their weight. Today this is impossible since mass production techniques require machine finishing of the ski. Weight is reduced by side channeling only. Most unfortunate of all is the loss of fine geometric characteristics of the hand-made wood ski now no longer available. Wood skis used to be dramatically "waisted" or side-cambered; that is, much broader at the tip and shovel than at the midpoint, and somewhat wider again at the tails. This made their tracking characteristics far superior to the modern virtually parallel sided ski which has replaced them. I am always buying old wooden touring skis, especially broad ones, whenever I see them. I have a friend who put a good looking old pair in the window of his shop just for decoration. A

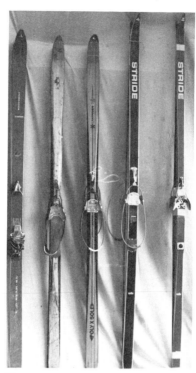

Figure 3.16 The Author's own Skis. (From left to right) Alpine Skis, Orienteering skis, Mountain Touring, Light Touring, and Racing Models.

customer offered him $50 for them, twice what they cost new! One used to be able to find good skis of this kind in the Salvation Army or Crippled Civilian Stores, but today many people are beginning to recognize that they are quite valuable.

Wood skis with hickory soles offer the best possible wax holding surface and, therefore, the fastest glide when purchase wax is used. The "P-tex" or polyethylene soles are also extremely fast, especially on wet snow and were used successfully by many racers at the 1976 Olympics in Innsbruck. Unquestionably synthetic bases are going to continue to gain in popularity for racers. I have many reservations about them for tour skiers who require more physical assistance from the ski in obtaining a good kick. Hickory is all imported from the U.S. by the European ski manufacturers and its cost is very high. Consequently many of the cheaper mass produced wooden skis use birch and beech for ski soles. These softer woods actually hold wax better than hickory but tend to wear out quickly when exposed to crusty ice conditions. Many of the cheap skis being imported are quite inferior products. I've often gone through a dozen pairs in a shop not finding one pair that wasn't badly warped!

The whole problem for the wood ski manufacturer is how to make a ski which is both rugged and light at the same time. Hardwoods (beech, ash, hickory, birch) are stronger than softwoods (spruce, pine, balsa) but are also heavier. Among the better wooden skis typical construction is four, five or six layers for a total of 20 to 36 laminations. A softwood core is sandwiched between laminations of hardwood. The sole is usually gouge-resistant hickory with lignostone (resin impregnated and compressed beechwood) edges for durability. Skis that skimp on laminations or do not contain the proper mix of hardwoods and softwoods are highly susceptible to warping, loss of camber, and quite commonly, excessive camber.

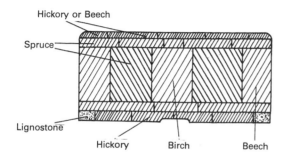

Hickory or Beech

Spruce

Lignostone

Hickory   Birch   Beech

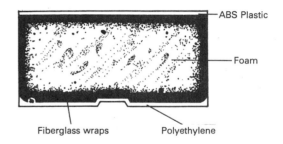

ABS Plastic

Foam

Fiberglass wraps   Polyethylene

Figure 3.17 These Touring Skis have lignostone edges. Note that the edges are wider and deeper on the "inside" of the skis.

Figure 3.17a Typical Ski Construction. Left: 5 Layer Laminated Wood Ski. Right: Fully Fibreglass Ski. Since the glass fibre reinforced plastic wraps around the core, a stiffer ski is produced. Sandwich construction without structural material on the sides of the ski is also available.

Figure 3.18 Lampinen Model 12 "Mountain" Touring Skis. An excellent choice for all around off-the-trail skiing. Bottoms are plastic impregnated beech.

Flex and Camber

Camber is the natural curve of the ski which assists in distributing the skier's weight over its length. It is positive when curved in a concave fashion towards the snow and negative in a convex fashion. Alpine skis traditionally flex in a uniform convex slope towards the snow when weighted. More weight is placed on the snow under the foot than at the tip and tails. Cross-country touring skis generally flex in a similar way but racing skis have what is termed *double camber* in that when weighted, their tips and tails actually turn up before the center of the ski starts to. We used to consider this characteristic a defect, but today it means the skier's weight is much more uniformly spread over the length of the ski maximizing his glide.

While the alpine skier gets good edge control directly beneath his feet where his skis are most heavily loaded, the cross-country racer has and needs minimal edge control there. If the skier's kick is not sufficiently strong to press the ski into the snow beneath his feet, he will also have terrible backslip. Racing skis are made in a vast variety of flexibilities and the buyer should make sure that he does not purchase a ski which demands more performance from his techniques than he can muster.

Most serious racers require several pairs of skis, each of a different flex for use on difficult courses where glide or kick must be stressed.

Excessive positive camber is a common problem in purchasing cross-country skis. Many cheaper skis tend to pick up positive camber in storage and when they are sold in the pre-season sales they are already useless. This is especially true for light adults and children who cannot depress the ski sufficiently to get good bite. So long as this is the case waxing is hopeless and they will be forever plagued with backslip. When the skis are held sole to sole there should be approx 1½ to 2 inches (38-50 mm) between them at the balance point where the binding is to be installed. It should be possible to squeeze the ski soles directly together at this point and have them meet over the entire length of both skis. Often when one does this one ski will stay partially curved indicating a differential in the stiffness of the skis or a poorly matched pair. When the skis are squeezed together in this way the tops should not spread. Be certain that the contact point between the skis stays in the same place as you bring them together. One way to check that the amount of flex is proper is to place the skis on the floor with a piece of paper underneath the boot position, stand on them, distributing your weight equally to each ski, and have a second person try to pull the paper out. There should be some friction resisting its withdrawal but not significantly more friction than at the tip and tail of the ski. If the paper pulls out easily the ski is too stiff for the individual. If the paper cannot be withdrawn it is too flexible. This is a somewhat crude method for determining the flex of one's ski, but unless an expert is available who can accurately assess the characteristics of the ski, it is perhaps the best.

Length

Cross-country skis are manufactured in lengths from children's skis to adult sizes of 160 cm to 220 cm or more, generally in 5 cm increments. Selecting the proper length is usually done by picking a ski whose tip comes to the center of the palm of one's hand when bent at 90° at the wrist, the arms held over the head, the heels firmly on the floor. People who are extra heavy for their height should go 5 cm larger, and if extra light, 5 cm shorter. This is a rough guide but usually adequate. Another factor I consider important is length of legs relative to over all height. Remarkable variations occur in people. If one has very long legs but a short upper body one might well end up with skis which are too short relying solely on the arm length guide. I prefer to select the ski by standing on the skis in the telemark position (see (p. 87) with the boots carefully placed relative to the balance point see p. 88) . If the skis are the right length the tip of the trailing one will exactly touch the ankle bone of the forward foot.

Blocking one ski against the other always involves some risk that one will "over power" the other and mis-match them. It is therefore very wise to store your skis clamped against a flat wall.

Figure 3.19 Proper Ski length.

Which ski to choose?

As you can see the business of finding the right ski is not very easy. After you have determined the width and weight type based on your skiing intentions, you still have to decide on material, soles, and flex *and* be wary of flex/camber problems.

From the material standpoint, wood has the advantage of inherently having a superior sole surface. The synthetics on the other hand have superior strength stability and flex/camber characteristics. I would suggest that the latter is more critical for the athletic skier and the racer, and less so for the tour skier. My prejudice against the fibreglass or synthetic ski is gradually on the wane from a material standpoint. My complaints about modern skis are really restricted to their geometry.

As for the choice in soles, I favour natural hickory first. It may well be that the synthetics will soon rival it. Waxing synthetic soles (see Chapter Six) is quite a different problem and one I have little experience with. I do know that wax applied with heat lasts longer and one is restricted in the use of heat with the synthetics. The resin or oil impregnated wood soles are a good compromise in that their wax holding ability is quite good and you can use a torch on them with care!

No-wax soles whether positive or negative, diamonds, mohair, or fish scale, all sacrifice some glide speed for the purchase, or bite, they provide. Additionally the positive type fish scale soles are very noisy.

ALL ABOUT POLES

Poles range from tonkin bamboo cane priced at $5 to $10, to carbon fibre "butterfly" or "hoof" basket, carbide tipped racing poles priced at well over $100. In between these extremes there are fibreglass poles and high-strength aluminum alloy poles priced between $16 and $35. The ski poles must be looked upon as an expendable piece of equipment to the cross-country skier. Inevitably he will fall and break or bend a pole if he is an active skier. Therefore, to invest such large sums in these new sophisticated poles, I feel, is folly, except for the dedicated racer. Tonkin cane, the cheapest of the materials, is grown in Indochina and is extremely light, strong and far and away the superior choice for poles. Important considerations when buying a pole are: type of

Figure 3.20 Negative waxless ski bottoms: (On the left) *steps have been machined into plastic surface;* on the right, *diamonds have been molded into it.*

Positive waxless ski bottoms: (On the left) *molded fish scales project, more so in the kick portion than in the glide portion.* On the right, *mohair strips are inserted in the kick portion.*

Figure 3.21 Proper pole length.

Some-how that is a feature no cross-country skier around should need! I consider all of the no-wax soles *too* big a compromise. But then, they may be suitable for some people who don't care about their speed at all and refuse to mess with any wax. The fish scales and step type can be sanded out with a belt sander (use care!) if you already have some and want to get rid of them.

basket, length of pole, and type of grip. If you intend to ski in deep snow often, under soft powder conditions, a large size basket is extremely important. The small diameter ones intended for racing will sink into the snow too easily, offering too little resistance when the pole is pushed. If you are an active racer you may be interested in the butterfly basket, an asymmetrical design which prevents the basket from dragging in the snow when it is withdrawn during the diagonal stride. A perceptible amount of energy normally wasted, is conserved thereby. Special large diameter baskets can be bought separately for ski mountaineering use.

The length of the pole should be approximately the same for all types of skiing although racers use longer poles for courses with a lot of flat ground and shorter ones when there are many hills. The popular length brings the tip of the pole into the armpit when standing with the basket on the snow. To judge the length when purchasing a pole in a shop, turn the pole upside down and stand it vertically on the floor. The basket should come approximately even with the armpit.

The type of grip is important. Materials available are generally cork, leather, and synthetic plastic. Either of the first two I find quite satisfactory. I would not recommend the synthetic material as it does not absorb moisture, can cause one's hands to become cold, and tends to slip in the glove-clad hand. Be certain that you purchase a pair of poles which have adjustable wrist straps. This is very important if you ski throughout the year and will be varying the covering on your hands depending on the weather. I find in the spring that I often ski without gloves at all; while in the early part of the winter I may have heavy woollen mittens and leather shell covers. The

Figure 3.22 Pole Grips. (Left to right) *Rutter Alpine Type (Scott-U.S.A.) aluminium shaft, Leather Racing Type (Karhu) fibreglass shaft, Cork Touring (Scott-U.S.A.) aluminum shaft, Plastic Touring (Splitkein) tonkin cane, Leather Touring (Liljedahl) tonkin cane.*

difference in bulk requires a different length adjustment on the wrist strap for the hand to fit comfortably just below the top of the grip portion of the pole (see Figure 5.2 on p. 66). Approximately $1/2$ inch (13 mm) of the shaft should project above the fingers when the pole is gripped.

The fibreglass poles have often shown a tendency to be brittle under extremely cold conditions. If one strikes a tree sharply while

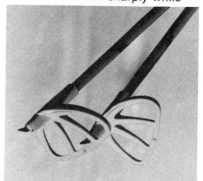

Figure 3.23 "Butterfly" or "Hoof" Racing Basket. *Assymmetrical design prevents it from dragging in the snow when being withdrawn.*

skiing in the woods, this kind of pole may shatter. The ideal basket for deep snow touring has yet to be devised. Years ago one could obtain them fabricated of leather straps riveted to a very light bamboo hoop. This type no longer exists, undoubtedly due to its high fabrication costs. Today's are molded in synthetic rubber and are quite heavy. If one visualizes the weight which must be picked from the snow and swung forward during the diagonal stride, one can really see that every fraction of an ounce that can be removed from the end of the pole is going to be of assistance. For this reason, I would not advise buying the very large basket unless one does a large amount of very deep snow skiing where steep ascents must be made. Top line racing poles include the Exel "Grafil Champion" (under 300 grams (10½ oz.), Liljedahl "Racer", and Moon model 125. Good aluminum and tonkin cane poles are made by many manufacturers, notably Liljedahl, Jofa, Normark, and Nyberg.

ALL ABOUT ACCESSORIES

Ski accessories required for cross-country skiing are really very few. *Waxes* are covered in Chapter Six. A rucksack for carrying your lunch and/or emergency gear; some goggles if you are going near brush or in the bright sun; and other incidentals for the longer or off-trail tour such as map and compass, spare ski tip and the like, are all that you need.

Rucksacks range upwards from a nylon $3.95 variety which zips into a small packet the size of a package of cigarettes. This type will do for one or two people on a short tour. I prefer a standard day pack or "summit" pack which can hold a load of up to 12 lbs (5.4 kg) or more if necessary. Mine weighs about 18 oz (510 g) and has a single compartment with a zippered pocket in the flap. It has a leather patch on the back for tying on crampons or other sharp objects. Many good ones such as the Millet "Jannu 521" or the Karrimor "Tatra" are on the market for $15 to $35. This kind of rucksack will enable one person to carry lunch and emergency clothing for a family of 4 on all day tours without much difficulty. Avoid belt packs or fanny packs used by Alpine Ski Patrolmen. These are very restricting on your waist and place a cantilevered load just where you don't need it. For ski tours involving extra equipment such as a climbing rope and hardware, a somewhat larger rucksack such as the Millet "Le Freney 165" or Karrimor "Aiquille" would be a better choice.

Figure 3.24 Rucksacks for cross-country skiing. Bergan's Model (right) allows attachment of skis, ice axe, crampons, etc. Style on the left is ideal for general touring. Belt pack in foreground is not recommended.

(Left to Right) Ultima Thule "soft" pack by Chouinard, Kelty Tour pack, Karrimor "Joe Brown", and "Chamonix" by Millet.

Any rucksack should be fitted with a waist strap so that it can be held snug to your body and not swing on your back when turning. Absorbent cotton or insulated backs are a good feature as well. Leather bottoms are superbly tough but very heavy. Vinyl will do equally well. The all-nylon bottoms wet through rather quickly in the snow. Shoulder straps should be well padded and connected to the pack at the top close together so they don't slide off your shoulders.

Much of the comfort when using a small rucksack depends upon your packing job. Line the surface against your back with soft clothing and spread it out so that the load doesn't lump into a single ball. The object is to get the load as close to your center of gravity as possible. Don't put breakables such as a camera on the outside where they can be damaged in a spill. For this reason, carrying a camera in a rucksack is usually pointless as you never bother to rummage through to get it out. If you really want to take pictures, wear the camera on an elasticized chest harness just inside your anorak.

49

For ski mountaineering and overnight touring a "soft pack" large enough for your gear is needed. These are preferable to metal pack frames as the load is carried closer to your body. The Ultima "Thule" or Karrimor "Joe Brown" are excellent, although quite expensive ($80 to $100). Lowe Alpine Systems (LAS) make a popular "expedition" model which is reasonable in cost. Use of your soft pack for bivouac purposes should be considered. Many have an interior skirt that can be pulled out around you should you ever have to spend a night huddled in your rucksack! If I am going out on a quick tour, the odd tube of wax or chocolate bar can easily be carried in the chest pocket of my anorak. However when it comes to extra clothing, I would much rather put on a small rucksack than have anything tied around my waist.

Goggles such as the Uvex sun goggle is an excellent choice for most cross-country skiers. Made of unbreakable plastic with replaceable lenses, it is as totally open as sun glasses, allowing the ventilation demanded for cross-country use. At $15 a pair they are expensive but I have seen cheaper copies for about half that amount. I wear mine while bushwacking, but probably conventional alpine goggles are better. Take a razor knife and cut out as much of the rubber frame as possible to improve ventilation. The sense of security for your eyes which a good pair of goggles provides as you crash through the bush on skis, makes them well worth it.

In the mountains above timberline you will need glacier glasses such as Cebe "Eiger" or Julbo mountaineering glasses. Unfortunately due to the necessary side protectors most glacier glasses do fog up if you are exerting yourself strenuously. Always carry an emergency pair of goggles when above timberline. I have a pair of simple folding cloth-frame and celluloid ones which weigh virtually nothing.

Compasses for day tour survival use can be pretty minimal items. However I prefer to carry a good orienteering compass such as the Silva "Ranger" or "Safari" models which facilitate sighting bearings. They weight about 3 oz and cost between $12 and $25. Don't forget the map you will need to use the compass effectively!

Figure 3.26 Good Compasses for ski touring. Left, Silva "Ranger"; right, "Safari".

Cameras for use on ski tours should be super light, compact, and indestructable. The Minox 35 EL (around $180) is a full frame 35 mm fully automatic camera which is ideal for ski touring and mountaineering. It fits in your shirt pocket, weighs around 8 oz (226 g) and has a plastic case which folds to conceal its superb lens. Camera experts currently rank it optically comparable to cameras costing $1000 or more!

Figure 3.25 Goggles for cross-country skiing. (Upper left) Glacier glasses; (upper right) Folding cloth frame Emergency Goggles – everyone should have a pair.
(Bottom) Uvex Cross-Country Glasses. Good for general trail skiing and bushwacking. Use an elastic strap.

Spare Ski Tips are essential for the longer tour where they may save you a long and very awkward walk. At least one person in every group should carry one. Make sure that it is adjustable such as the Nortur aluminum hinged tip ($6); or if it is not adjustable I recommend the Dovre or Rex plastic tips. Make sure it will fit every ski in the party. NORS*QUIP (see below) make an adjustable ski tip which incorporates a saw as well. Sometimes fitting a spare tip on the splintered end of a broken ski can be tricky. Make sure your basic rucksack kit always contains a jack knife!

Climbing Skins, sometimes called sealskins, are not essential but extremely useful for glacier skiing or touring ascents especially on firm snow. Skins are generally not used in powder. To be effective you must ascend straight up the fall line as a traverse causes the skins to slip sideways. I would use them primarily on firm snow on a glacier or snow field where I wished to avoid the added crevasse risk of being on foot carrying my skis.

Models are made for both touring skis and alpine skis. Costs run between $40 and $50.

Figure 3.28 ''Vinersa'' Climbing Skins. About $50.

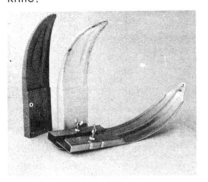

Figure 3.27 Spare Tips for touring. Plastic models are non-adjustable but very light. Aluminum models are heavier but will fit any width ski. Type shown with two fastening screws generally is easier to attach to broken ski.

NORS*QUIP, 432 Porter Ave., Buffalo, N.Y. 14201

SOURCES FOR EQUIPMENT

Finding cross-country equipment has each year become less and less of a problem (unless you are a fanatic like myself searching out super-wide skis!). Since most ski shops stock a relatively small number of brands or lines, I recommend that you acquire the catalogues of the major wilderness supply houses. You will find these volumes crammed with useful information. From them you can isolate the types of equipment you want and then look for it locally. Often actually purchasing through the mail is practical and economical. Postage is often offset by the avoidance of a local sales tax.

Skis are tricky but all other items are no problem at all.

I list below some of the best sources of cross-country equipment and their speciality. Write for their catalogues and carefully compare characteristics such as weight before ordering. Some may make a nominal charge for their catalogue but it is well worth it.

Clothing:

East
LL Bean Inc.,
746 Main St.,
Freeport, Maine
04033

Eddie Bauer Inc.,
22 Bloor Street W.,
Toronto, Ontario.
M4W 1A1

Black's International,
3525 Queen Mary Rd.,
Montreal, Québec H3V 1H9

West
Eddie Bauer Inc.,
Third and Virginia,
Seattle, Washington.

Sierra Designs,
4th and Addison Streets,
Berkeley, California.
94710

The Ski Hut,
P.O. Box 309
1615 University Ave.,
Berkeley, Calif., 94701

Rucksacks:

Overseas
Karrimor,
Avenue Parade,
Accrington, BB5 6PR
Lancashire, England

also: ABC Recreational Equipment above.

Skis, Boots, Bindings and Poles:

East
Eastern Mountain Sports Inc.,
1041 Commonwealth Ave.,
Boston, Mass.
02215

Aker's Ski
Andover, Maine, 04216

Margesson's Ltd.,
17 Adelaide St. E.,
Toronto, Ont. M5C 1H4

Moor and Mountain Inc.,
67 Main St.,
Concord, Massachusetts

West
Recreational Equipment Co.,
P.O. Box 22090,
Seattle, Wash. 98122

Overseas

Gresvig Sport,
Oslo, Norway

Tents and Sleeping Bags:

West
The North Face,
1234 Fidth St.,
Berkeley, Calif. 94710

ABC Recreational Equipment,
555 Richards St.,
Vancouver, B.C.
V6B 225

Midwest
Holubar,
Box 7,
Boulder, Colo. 80302

Ski Mountaineering Specialties:

Overseas
Sporthous Schuster,
Munich, Germany

West
Liberty Mountain Sports,
P.O. Box 306,
Montrose, Calif. 91020

also: Recreational Equipment Co. Seattle (See above)

Racing Equipment (also trail markers, timers, bibs, roller skis, etc.)

East
Reliable Racing Supply,
624 Glen St.,
Glen Falls, New York 12801

Should you not find enough above, buy a copy of *"Nordic Skiing"* Magazine, P.O. Box 106 West Brattleboro, Vermont, 05301. It contains much interesting information as well as many sources for equipment.

Another excellent source reference is *"SKI INFO"* $5.95 from Forest Publications Inc., 20 Hill St., Morristown, New Jersey 07960. In this single reference, 99% of all skis, poles, and boots, manufactured worldwide are listed with their vital statistics!

Another interesting magazine is *"Nordic World"*. Write P.O. Box 366, Mountain View , California 94042 for more information.

In every metropolitan area there are now dozens of ski and sport shops which sell cross-country equipment. However, usually there is one which was there first and has, consequently, superior experience. Following is perhaps the *most* incomplete list in this book, but if you haven't visited the listed shop closest to you, you should.

East

New York City

Scandinavian Ski and Sport Shop,
40 West 57th St.
N.Y.C. New York
(212) 757-8524

Boston

Eastern Mountain Sports,
1041 Commonwealth Ave.
Boston, Mass.
(617) 254-4250

Montreal

Siren Ski Shop,
6131 Sherbrooke St. W.
Montreal, Quebec
(514) 482-2734

Andover, Maine

Akers Ski Shop,
"behind the post office",
Andover, Maine
(207) 392-4582

Toronto

Margesson's
17 Adelaide St. E.,
Toronto, Ontario
(416) 362-2721

West

Seattle

Recreational Equipment Co.,
11th Ave and East Pine St.,
Seattle, Washington
(206) 323-8333

Vancouver

ABC Recreational Equipment,
1822 West 4th Ave.,
Vancouver, B.C.
(604) 731-4081

CHAPTER FOUR
CLOTHING FOR CROSS-COUNTRY SKIING

I used to say, "One of the nice things about cross-country skiing is that you can wear anything". Well, that was true when alpine skiers were dressing in incredible outfits and cross-country buffs were just out there in their jeans. Nothing has changed really; the alpine skiers have more elaborate outfits than ever, and the new super chic cross-country "outfits" aren't selling that well. However, I am increasingly conscious of the large number of people who go out cross-country skiing dressed too warmly. Today everyone has a down parka and, because it seems nice and light, everyone assumes that it will be appropriate. What most people fail to realize is that exercise produces a tremendous amount of heat. Unless conditions are quite severe, clothing one wears indoors in a cool house is all that is required to stay comfortable outside, as long as one is moving.

The down vests which are now so popular are not bad. One is less apt to perspire in a vest than in a parka since vests provide periodic ventilation through the arm holes.

Time and again I see people in heavy ski parkas and warm-up pants shuffling along. If they were to move any faster they would expire! I like to dress so that I am on the cool side and am forced to keep moving in order to keep warm. It is extremely important, however, to always have emergency clothing on hand. Even in good weather, on a short family ski tour, I carry enough clothing so that, if necessary, two people could remain outside standing still and be reasonably comfortable for a couple of hours. So long as I have this much with me, I encourage the others to wear as little as possible. Under-dressing a novice skier or a small child can be a mistake however, as they will quite naturally exercise less, and therefore generate less heat.

I like to dress in a way which enables me to make small adjustments depending on conditions. In other words I wear several thin layers which can easily be removed or added to as I get hotter or colder.

Figure 4.2 The Author's son Ben dressed comfortably for a tour on a cold but calm day.

Body heat is usually radiated approximately as follows:
   40% from the head;
   20% from the hands and wrists;
   10% from the feet; and
   30% from the body core and legs.
In extreme cold conditions or "survival" circumstances it is very important to force excess heat off through the body core; in other words, to always keep the head and hands covered. Once the body core is allowed to cool, hypothermia results (see "cold injuries", Chapter Eight). Consequently, if one becomes overheated in extreme cold conditions, one should ventilate the body trunk or torso by opening a jacket at the throat rather than by removing one's hat.

In milder conditions where there is reasonable assurance that you are not going to become over-chilled, quite the reverse is true. I regularly ski without hat or gloves in temperatures down to 20° or 25°F (–4°C to –7°C). The heat lost through these "radiators" prevents my body core from becoming overheated.

Keeping Dry. Another problem with dressing for skiing is keeping dry. Wet clothing conducts the body heat away, leaving you cold and very miserable. Moisture comes from three sources; melting of snow which clings to clothing, precipitation, and perspiration.

The problem of snow clinging to clothing is particularly acute when skiing in very deep powder snow, or for a beginner taking many tumbles. Never brush the snow off your knee socks. This promotes melting of the snow and forces it into the sock. The light fluffy layer of snow which gathers on the outside actually forms an insulation layer, if not disturbed. Generally, gaiters made of a light woven fabric (which does not accumulate snow) eliminate this problem. Avoid bulky woolen sweaters which can accumulate snow.

Having a relatively waterproof parka, certainly one that is windproof, is essential in a snowstorm if you hope to remain dry. Mine is quite baggy and tends to shield my knickers from falling snow and even rain. It has a hood which can be drawn up tightly around the face to prevent snow getting down my neck.

Figure 4.1 The Annual Washington's Birthday Race, Putney, Vermont.

Moisture from perspiration is perhaps the most difficult problem to deal with. It can be solved through the process of absorption and evaporation. Brynje or net type underwear creates a very thin layer of air next to the skin. This layer, when warmed, provides an insulation value similar to the air space in insulating window glass. When chilled, the body tries to form this air space naturally by creating "goose pimples". The air space allows perspiration to evaporate before it soaks through one's clothes. Over the rest of the body one must rely on the absorptive value of our clothing to soak away perspiration. I like all-cotton turtleneck shirts next to my skin with several layers of cotton flannelette shirts on top. For the feet, I've always used woollen athletic socks beneath my heavy woollen knicker socks. Light cotton, or silk wick socks are also very good.

In summary then, clothing for cross-country skiing should "breathe", it should be light-weight, it should keep you dry, and it should stop the wind.

In the following pages I will describe in detail the various items of clothing available and will also recommend sources for them.

For information on, and a list of distributors for excellent cross-country skiing socks write:
Wigwam Mills Inc.,
Sheboggan, Wisconsin 53081
or,
Hanson Mills Ltd.,
Hull, Québec

SOCKS

There is no substitute for thick wool socks when wearing knickers. I prefer the thermal type (which are smooth on the outside and less likely to accumulate snow) to the more loosely-knit variety. I wear regular woollen athletic socks underneath, but many people prefer light-weight cotton wick socks as these draw off the moisture and lessen the chances of cold feet. The total sock thickness should be approximately equal to two pairs of medium-weight woollen socks. Avoid the traditional ornamentally ribbed knee socks which provide more surface for snow to cling to.

Figure 4.3 Socks for skiing: (1) thermal type knee sock; (2) ribbed knee sock; (3) athletic sock; (4) thermal liner sock; (5) Cotton wick sock.

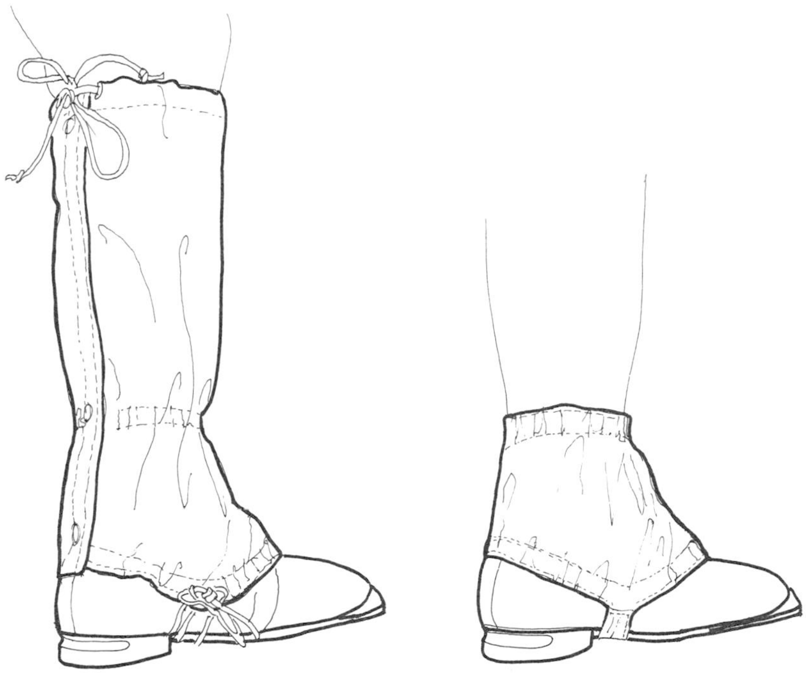

GAITERS AND ANKLETS

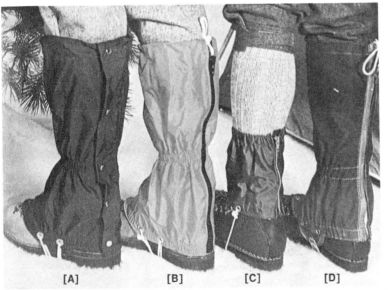

Figure 4.4 Gaiters and anklets.

Due to the low cut nature of most cross-country ski boots, and since the boot is not covered in any way when wearing knickers and knee socks, it is necessary to use gaiters or anklets to keep snow from getting into the boot. Gaiters are full knee-length outer coverings for the boot and knee socks, securely fastened to the boot and fitted with an elasticized seal around the knee. I nearly always ski with gaiters. I use the simpler anklets only when I know I will not ski in any deep snow.

The gaiter must have a well flared bottom which will thoroughly cover all of the boot laces and generally fit the shape of the boot. The best type have a hook on the front which can be inserted under the first lace, and grommets on each side for use with laces under the instep to hold it firmly down. If the gaiter is constructed properly, no snow will penetrate to the upper of the boot and you will arrive home with nice dry laces to untie. I use leather boot laces beneath the instep since these last longer than the usual cotton laces. The top of the gaiter should reach the top of the knee and be hemmed with a draw string. Elasticized tops alone are not adequate to hold the gaiter up. I tie mine above the knee buckle on my knickers, covering the joint between knicker and socks, and they never slip down.

Figure 4.5 Gaiter types available from the Recreational Equipment Co. Type "B" is best for skiing.

[A]   [B]   [C]   [D]

Figure 4.6 Coated nylon anklet – ideal for most trail touring.

Gaiters should be made of sturdy canvas duck, or of a nylon which breathes easily. I find the canvas duck to be superior to nylon in its water-proofing properties although it is a little heavier in weight. Gaiters are made with zippers up the back so that they can be put on after the boots. This is an essential feature in the heavier canvas ones, but the lighter nylon models can easily be pulled on over one's knee socks before putting on the boots. Many gaiters on the market are not sufficiently flared at the bottom to properly fit the boot, and therefore, either leave some laces exposed, or get all bunched up around the ankle. Some are made of rubberized nylon and do not breathe properly; others are made of cheap cotton and soak through quickly.

Costs today (1977) range anywhere from $8 to $20. I recommend getting a good pair for they should last you many years. I also use mine mountaineering, fitting them over my climbing boots. When ski mountaineering they protect half of your leg against the wind, often enabling you to dispense with wind pants. The best thing about gaiters, aside from the way they keep you dry, is that you can put them on over any old pair of trousers and presto, you are ready to ski! When there is a blizzard I can travel to my office on skis. I put them on over my suit! At other times, I can be ready to ski in seconds simply by slipping on my gaiters and boots. Really, there is no more useful item to own than gaiters.

Figure 4.7 The author skiing to the office in downtown Toronto during a blizzard. Gaiters and an anorak are all that are required to convert a business suit into a skiing outfit.

UNDERWEAR

People vary tremendously in their need for long underwear while skiing. When I wear my corduroy knickers, I seldom bother with long johns of any sort unless it is below zero and windy. If I'm wearing light poplin knickers, I use an old pair of very thin cotton long johns which are cut off at the knee. Downhill skiers assume that long underwear should be worn for cross-country when often it is not necessary.

The "brynje" or Scandinavian "open net" uppers and lowers are generally considered the best for keeping warm and keeping dry. I have some, but I don't often wear them preferring instead the smooth cotton variety if conditions are cold enough. If you are racing and perspiring a lot, the "brynje" is unquestionably better than the smooth cotton. Correspondingly, if you are ski mountaineering and/or in circumstances where you must be dressed for a possible bivouac, then the "open net" is definitely a better choice (Figure 4-8).

Underwear is always worn directly against the skin where it can create an insulative air layer. Wearing anything underneath it will completely negate its value. Buy it slightly on the large side as it will shrink somewhat. Your other clothing will press it against your body in any event. Very tight-fitting brynje leaves you striped with red welts all over, and quite uncomfortable!

Cotton underwear is available nearly everywhere. "Duofold" is one of the better brands, but quite expensive. Brynje net-type underwear is also available in most ski shops today. I wear a net-type top with a cotton bottom most often and would recommend purchasing such a combination.

Figure 4.8 "Brynje" or net underwear.

KNICKERS, TROUSERS AND SKIRTS

Almost everyone agrees that knickers allow the most freedom of movement for cross-country skiing. These vary in weight from heavy wool and corduroy to extremely light cotton, poplin, and synthetic-type fabrics like Lycra. The heavy-weight are designed for mountaineering use but are still very good for tour skiing and a requirement for ski mountaineering. Light-weight knickers are good for racing or fast touring on a trail. They may not stand the abuse of bushwacking in the woods. Today, knickers are available everywhere so there is no problem. However, I still rate them secondary in importance to gaiters, since with gaiters one can wear any type of trousers. I have a pair of cavalry twill trousers which are very warm and which I find excellent for the purpose.

Figure 4.9 Jacket/knicker cross-country suits made of stretch type synthetic fabrics are very comfortable. Costs range from $25 to $75.

Figure 4.10 Skiing in a skirt.

In the past, women often skied in skirts. For some reason this is rare today, and I think it's too bad. Especially since pantyhose and leotards are now available to keep one warm. Somehow, linked double telemarks, arm in arm, with some clothing distinction between sexes would be better!

SHIRTS, SWEATERS, ANORAKS.

In the shirt and sweater area, nearly everything is appropriate so long as it is warm and light-weight. I like cotton turtlenecks and flannelette shirts under light woollen sweaters. These plus an anorak are all one needs in temperatures down to 15° to 20° F (–7°C to –9°C) (assuming light winds).

The anorak, or wind protective outer shell, is one of the most important items of cross-country clothing. Skiing without a parka, when conditions are comfortable for it, is ideal. But when the cold, wind, or precipitation demand more protection, a high quality parka should be your first priority. A good parka will last many years and I would rather have it than a fancy down-filled jacket. I've used my World War Two ski troop surplus anorak for 20 years now, wearing it in all kinds of severe conditions, and it has proved excellent. Some

GLOVES AND MITTENS

This is also an area where personal requirements vary dramatically. Light cotton work gloves, the kind available in any hardware store for 69¢, serve me very well under most conditions. But I am careful to see that they don't get wet! Others might freeze in them. For protection against simple abrasion from the ski poles, they are excellent. Racers use specially ventilated gloves designed for the purpose.

For cold weather, I recommend a plain woollen mitten inside a light deerskin outer shell. Gloves give a much better "feel" for the pole but I do not think they are essential. Pole movement in cross-country skiing should be quite relaxed and mittens seem OK to me. Good wool mittens and a pair of light leather shells will cost approximately $15. Fancy $30 down-filled mittens or gloves used by alpine skiers are not appropriate. Personally, I don't keep as warm in them as I do in the woollen mitts anyway, and their sheer bulk is awkward for cross-country skiing. New, quick drying gloves (for use inside mittens) are supposed to be good. Versions made in silk are particularly good. Photographers often use these for handling cameras in cold weather.

Figure 4.11 Ventile fabric used by Black's in making this excellent anorak and knickers combination has superb wind and weatherproof characteristics and still breathes.

people prefer a knee-length anorak or "cagoule" for extremely foul weather. A "cagoule" can serve as your own personal tent in the event of a bivouac but is inappropriate for everyday hiking.

Normally, outer wind parkas range from the light nylon "shell" which is really only a wind proof shirt, to the proper anorak with a hood sufficiently large to be worn over a heavy sweater or light down jacket. The nylon shell is great for short cross-country tours. It can be crushed to a size that will fit in your pocket. Of more general use,

however, is the anorak. Generally, these are made of poplin or some good breathing material. Black's of Goodenough, England, manufacture one in their, "Ventile" fabric which is excellent.

Figure 4.12 Gloves for skiing: (1) cotton work gloves; (2) deerskin shells with wool mittens; (3) XC Racing gloves. (These sometimes require cotton or Acrylic liner); (4) NASA developed thermal liner gloves; (5) downfilled alpine ski mitts

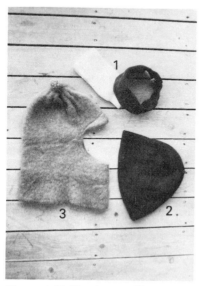

Figure 4.13 Headgear: (1) headbands; (2) standard tuque; (3) balaclava (wool also available in silk and synthetic fabrics).

HEADGEAR

As the number one radiator of body heat, the head offers a perfect means of controlling over-all temperature under normal conditions. This is why I normally ski without a hat. As I get colder, I put on an earband which protects my ears but still allows a lot of heat to escape through the top. If this proves inadequate, I use a woollen toque which can be pulled down over the ears and neck. If this is still inadequate, I raise my anorak hood and tie it around my face. The last resort is to wear a heavy woollen balaclava which can be pulled over the chin as well. I normally carry a balaclava amongst my emergency clothing. I have been in many extreme emergency situations and the balaclava has always kept me

warm. Silk balaclavas, popular with motor cyclists, are excellent since they take so little space and yet, are so warm. Some people who cannot stand the chafing of wool balaclavas wear a silk one underneath. Remember to keep your head fully covered at all times in a survival situation. Also, ventilate your body core at the throat by opening a parka or shirt *before* removing your headgear.

Headbands cost from $2.00 - $ 5.00
Toques cost from $5.00 - $15.00
Balaclavas cost from $6.00 - $10.00

EMERGENCY CLOTHING

In my rucksack, I usually carry emergency clothing for at least two people in the party. However, everyone in the group should ideally fend for themselves and have the following items in addition to what I have described above:

Windpants are very light nylon or poplin windproof pants and can be crumpled into a very small space. These are purposely made large so that they can easily slip over ski boots, and even over climbing boots with crampons on them! Some have a zipper on the side to make this easier. I use mine when it starts to rain. This is one item which needs relatively little "breathing" capability. Even the rubberized nylon rain-gear pants work quite well although they are usually heavier than they need be. Costs for windpants range between $15 and $30.

Figure 4.14 Good Emergency Clothing for your rucksack: (1) Down sweater; (2) Wool shirt; (3) Dry socks; (4) Dry mittens; (5) Windpants.

Down Sweaters is the term usually applied to a light-weight down-filled parka designed to be worn under an anorak. They also crush into a tiny space and are extremely warm. Costs for down sweaters range between $30 and $50. Often, down-filled underwear tops will do the job as well, but are only a little cheaper ($25). A good quality down sweater and anorak combination is as warm as a far bulkier "expedition weight" down parka.

Dry Socks are handy.

Plastic Bags take no space whatever but are remarkably serviceable as emergency gloves, socks, etc. Once I lost a glove in a high wind off the side of a mountain and used my lunch bag to cover my bare hand. I was amazingly comfortable! A sock can also double easily as a mitten.

All of the clothing which I've discussed in this chapter is suitable for all kinds of cross-country skiing. Obviously, the amount and nature of the actual garments selected will reflect anticipated temperatures, winds, and whether or not precipitation is likely.

For skiing under extreme weather conditions, and for any over-night outing the clothing selected must be supplemented, as I have said, by a warm parka, preferably down-filled. Many people have a tendency to think that an entirely different wardrobe is required for camping or ski mountaineering. This is not so. The point is that when active, the lightest clothing will do. When inactive, normal emergency clothing should do the job except under extreme conditions when the shelter of a cabin, tent, or igloo should be sought.

Learn to dress comfortably and most of all, learn to keep dry when skiing. These are the key clothing requirements for enjoying cross-country skiing.

CHAPTER FIVE
TECHNIQUE FOR CROSS-COUNTRY SKIING

The actual skiing techniques required for all forms of cross-country skiing are extremely similar. However, I would rank the types of cross-country skiing as follows in order of difficulty, or level of experience required:

1. Recreational Trail Touring
2. Deep Snow Touring
3. Orienteering
4. Mountain and Glacier Skiing
5. Competition

In this chapter I will cover all manoeuvers required for skiing on the level, climbing, and descending. Each may be practiced on the full range of equipment and variety of terrain associated with each type of skiing described in Chapter One with the qualification that mountain skiing, as discussed here, assumes the use of touring equipment and not alpine or downhill skiing equipment. It is a fundamental assumption here that no stemming, or forcing of the ski sideways through the snow, is used with touring equipment. This type of manoeuver, to me, demands alpine skis with steel edges and a rigid type binding. Light-weight touring skis would wear out rapidly, their edges become rounded and their bindings loosened if they were used in this way. There are some that prefer to ski deep powder using parallel technique on cross-country skis. To me this seems to be a mis-direction as it is so much more fun doing telemarks, *or* more fun on alpine skis. I love downhill skiing *and* mountain skiing with alpine equipment as well, but the technique must fall beyond the scope of this book.

Put on your skis then, and let's practice the fundamentals which will make it possible to explore all the variations of cross-country skiing which I have been talking about. When putting on your skis pick a good flat spot and arrange the skis left by right with your poles firmly planted on each side. The toe iron for all types of touring bindings slants more acutely away from the ski on the outside just as the sole of your boot does, thus making it easy to tell left from right. Clean the snow from the binding and the sole of your boot and place your foot carefully in the toe iron. With pin bindings be careful to align the boot with the pins, bringing the boot straight down on them. With cable bindings, slide the boot into the toe iron from the rear until it is snug. The "bail" on the pin binding need not be forced down excessively; all that is needed is a bit of pressure to keep the pins engaged. Likewise on cable bindings it should not require great force to keep the boot snugly in the toe iron held there by the sole lugs on each side. When people have problems with their skis coming off repeatedly, it is usually because there is snow beneath their boot and/or the toe iron is not properly aligned with the ski and boot.

MOVING ON THE LEVEL

When beginning to ski one should always start on the level. Acquiring a natural feeling standing on skis takes time. I maintain that one can tell an experienced skier simply by the way he stands on his skis. It takes time to relax, to be *more* comfortable on them than off them. Cross-country skis, whether they are super-light racing models, or the sturdier deep snow touring type, feel extremely light on your feet. To the alpine skier they seem featherweight by contrast. The totally unrestricted motion forward and backward is, at first, disconcerting. The first thing I teach rank beginners to do is to kneel on their skis and then roll on their side putting their skis over their heads. Note that the tips of the skis are heavier than the tails. When standing, if you pick up one foot, the tip will stay on the snow if you don't consciously lift it off. This is so your ski will stay in the track when you are gliding along and picking one ski entirely off the snow as you transfer your weight to the forward or gliding ski.

On flat ground with packed snow, experiment turning simply by stepping around. First move the tips of the skis one after another. Then try the same thing moving the tails in sequence.

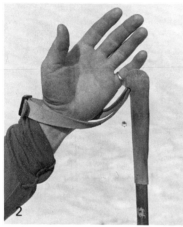

Figure 5.2 How to grip the pole. The wrist strap does the work allowing the hand clasp to be relaxed.

The Kick Turn

The first practical manoeuver to learn is the kick turn (see Figure 5.3). It is the simplest way in which to change direction. After you have mastered doing it on a steep hill you will be equipped to ski virtually any terrain!

First, on the level, kick one foot swiftly forward, allowing the tail of the ski to swing so that it may be planted firmly in the snow at right angles to the other ski's tip. The ski should be perfectly vertical, allowing it to be swung around easily and placed on the snow facing in the opposite direction as shown in the illustration. Then, pick up the other ski and bring it around alongside the first one. Your poles will seem to get in the way, so try it with no poles a few times. Ideally the poles should not be relied on for balance when doing the kick turn. Hence the importance of having your skis well planted in a precisely horizontal position. This will be even more important when you try it on a slope.

When you can do kick turns flawlessly on the flat without relying on your poles you are ready to try it on a small slope. Swing up and rotate the downhill ski first at all times. When you graduate to very steep hills this will be the only possible way of doing it. On a slope you may need to "edge" your skis into the slope a bit to prevent them from slipping. Always be certain that your skis are exactly perpendicular to the "Fall Line" (shortest and most direct line down the hill) before attempting the kick turn. As the hill steepens it becomes more and more necessary to brace oneself on the poles during the turn. Do not manoeuver both poles together. Keep one firmly planted at all times, so that you have it in place to brace against should the ski on the ground start to slide. It can be awkward to start sliding sideways just when you have both skis pointed in opposite directions!

Figure 5.3 The Kick Turn: Initiate the turn with a good swift kick to get your downhill ski into the Vertical Position (1). The rest is easy.

Figure 5.4 Having mastered the Kick Turn, you will be able to descend the
most difficult slopes simply by making very flat traverses, stopping and
reversing direction by means of the Kick Turn.

It is worthwhile to practice the kick turn as much as possible since it enables any skier to descend any slope simply linking them with a short downhill traverse.

Jumping in Place
An excellent way to improve your "feel" for the skis is to practice jumping vertically in place. Remove your poles and swing your arms to achieve more altitude. Alpine skiers will be amazed how much height they can achieve with the lightweight equipment. Try it with your poles and your height will be all the more amazing. I think any alpine "hot dogger", keen on aerobatics, could do truly amazing stunts on touring skis.

Figure 5.5 A variation of the Kick Turn. Quicker on Alpine Skis which are shorter.

The Step Turn

The next basic in-place manoeuver is the step turn. Like the kick turn it will find application later as you start descending hills. On the flat it can be done both forwards and backwards. Simply sit back slightly and move one ski at a time pushing off from one foot to the other as an ice skater does. Doing it in a backwards fashion, that is moving the tails of your skis rather than the tips, is faster for turning on the flat while stationary, but of little use when descending a hill! Try to develop a hopping motion in which you actually get both skis moving simultaneously.

Later when you learn to climb by sidestepping (see page 76) you will find that you can climb more rapidly by stepping around in this way.

snow, over bumps, ground obstacles, etc. Practicing *all* cross-country technique without poles at first is the best way to develop this instinct. The poles are a crutch for the recreational tour skier. Only for the racer are they vital. The beginning skier who strains on his poles for several hours will return home very sore in the shoulders!

Many of the techniques you will learn for descending slopes can be practiced effectively on the flat. When you go skiing and must wait for others in your party, don't stand still and get cold, keep moving. I am always moving on skis, even if on flat ground. Skate in circles, do summersaults, play fox and geese, do anything, but keep moving and you will never get cold or bored.

Figure 5.6 Stepping around on the flat.

The object of these exercises while standing still on your skis is to begin to exploit the full potential for movement; to relax and begin to be comfortable on skis. I have always maintained that a good skier should be able to climb a tree on skis! The expert cross-country skier must develop total control over the skis so as to be able to respond instinctively to changes in the

If you must rest, try sitting on a fencepost to get your feet off the snow. Don't take your skis off!

Moving Out

The great thing about cross-country is that anyone can go out and start sliding on the first day, without danger of falling, getting hurt, cold, or otherwise having a bad time of it. No matter how crippled you are if you can walk, you can ski. In fact I know a lot of people who can ski better than they can walk!

At first it is best for a beginner to start out on the flat in a broken trail made by other skiers. An ideal spacing for the tricks is about 6 inches between the skis. Many organized cross-country areas have trails in which these tracks have been mechanically grooved by a weighted sledge towed behind a snowmobile so that they are perfectly uniform and very easy for the beginner. The tracks prevent the skis from becoming crossed, precipitating loss of balance. The prepared track also has the advantage of a well packed surface in which to plant your poles.

The key to moving efficiently on the flat is in minimizing the amount of work the body must do while at the same time maximinzing the glide the skis give you on each stride. Gradually begin moving your stride from a simple walking shuffle to one in which your leg pendulums forward along with the opposite arm and you are able to kick off from the trailing leg and pole gliding out on the forward ski (Figure 5-9). This is the diagonal stride which forms the basis for all running on cross-country skis. Many people take up the sport enthusiastically and never even learn the diagonal stride. They prefer instead to simply shuffle along at their own pace. However, there is fantastic pleasure to be derived from getting a good stride and tearing along a well prepared trail. Developing a good stride is essential if you hope to ski long distances or at high speed.

Figure 5.7 Moving out on the flat – maximize glide; minimize effort.

Again, learning to stride is best done without poles. Drive the forward knee out, transferring the weight totally to the forward ski and getting it to slide further and further before swinging the opposite leg forward. Only when you can do this rhythmically and smoothly should you add your poles to further increase the effectiveness of your kick. Notice that as you drive your forward knee out in front of you, you must extend the opposite leg behind you to counter-balance yourself. Don't pick that trailing ski way off the snow as you see many skiers do. That serves no purpose and only tires you out.

Similarly, you will notice that as you drive the forward knee out, the opposite arm reaches back, a natural motion to all humans as they walk. In the diagonal stride you must exaggerate these natural motions and extend your body to maximize forward glide with minimum effort. Balance in the stride does not come easily. The further you extend yourself the more unstable you will be. It is

Figure 5.8 The skier must minimize all motions not essential to his forward travel.

Figure 5.9 Diagonal Stride without the use of poles. Note the accentuation of natural walking motions.

somewhat like balancing a bicycle, after trying and trying you suddenly find it easy and second nature. Balance while skiing is primarily achieved by equal and opposite motions – leg extensions and arm extensions fore and aft, diagonally together.

When you omit your poles you will find that the balancing act is easier to understand since the small poling force alongside that forward bent leg is often enough to throw the beginner completely off. Add this complexity only after you are quite ready. Figure 5-10 illustrates the complete diagonal stride sequence. Practice and critically review your body position in each phase. A few points of importance: (1) make all motions directly forward. Do not bob and weave at the waist. (2) Do not move your arms across your body. (3) Do not bend at the waist. Your body should be in a straight line – upper trunk and trailing leg, in each extension. (4) Look down the track, not at your feet. (5) Don't jump up and down on each stride; nothing will tire you more quickly as you are essentially doing on legged deepknee bends! Your head should stay virtually at one level above the snow throughout all phases of the stride. (6) Grip the poles loosely allowing them to swing on your wrist strap and opening your hand entirely at the end of each cycle. If you do not, not only will you not achieve as long a push, but you will also get cramps in your hands. Every effort should be made to conserve energy. A very good way to improve your diagonal stride is to watch experts. Go to races, better yet, *enter* a race and try to ski behind a good skier. Just as you learn alpine skiing by following a better skier, you will also learn cross-country technique by following trained racers.

Figure 5.10 The Diagonal Stride. A complete cycle from one leg to the other. Note erect upper body posture with the eyes looking down the track. Note pole planting position and sequence. Many skiers are plagued by getting their arms and legs out of sequence. Relax and think of your automatic motions during a quick walk. Now exaggerate these same motions and you will be doing the Diagonal Stride.

The tempo of your strides will vary with snow conditions; faster in slow snow, considerably slower in fast conditions when you are tempted to hang on to that glide for as long as possible.

Once you have perfected the diagonal stride it is only a matter of extending the period of time for which you can keep it up. Out on a lake, in a well prepared track, and with the proper wax you should feel like going on forever! Developing a powerful stride which you can maintain up hills is essential to the racer. I remember my amazement after years of racing as a teenager with *no* technique, in seeing a Norwegian trained racer maintain his stride directly up a considerable hill. Today virtually every competitor does.

Figure 5.11 (1) Completion of Left Ski Guide coincides with kick to start Right Ski Glide; (2) transition while gliding and poling to (3) Right Kick and Left Glide.

Double Poling is simply using both poles together either without striding, simply standing on your skis, or with a kick and stride at each stroke. Double poling is relaxing as a change of pace, and provides a useful variation on the diagonal stride. It is also the fastest way to travel on a slight downgrade, or even on the flat, under extremely fast conditions. Often a skier with poor purchase wax or no "bite" will end up double poling with no stride at all. This can become very tiring after even a short distance. Racers always double pole when starting down a hill in order to pick up speed quickly before going into a crouch.

Figure 5-13 illustrates all of the phases of simple double poling and Figure 5-14 illustrates double poling with a stride. Key points to watch are: (1) do not bend at the waist excessively. Upper trunk and ski poles should all be in a straight line. (2) Reach as far forward as possible in planting the poles and allow them to go as far behind you as possible maximizing the duration of thrust. (3) Retrieve the poles cleanly and allow them to pendulum forward again swinging between your thumb and index finger in a relaxed hand.

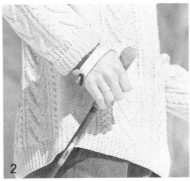

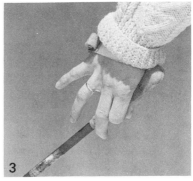

Figure 5.12 The Hand Grasp of the pole during the Diagonal Stride progresses from: (1) closed and firm at time of Pole Planting, to (2) relaxed while Pushing, to (3) open and relaxed when Withdrawing pole. In this way the hand does not become cramped.

Figure 5.13 Double Poling with a Stride. (1) the Beginning; (2) the Ending.

Double poling is very useful where the track is full of rolling ups and downs. One can push off from one bump and take a few strides up the next, push off from another and take a few strides up the next etc. It would be difficult to maintain a normal diagonal stride through such conditions. Sometimes with a strong tail wind it is possible to double pole for miles across a lake without too much strain. This is rare however. Most of the time double poling takes its toll on the upper body quite rapidly. The amount of force which is practical to expend through the poles is very minimal. Unlike legs which are conditioned to carry your weight for hours on end, the arms and shoulders have far less endurance. Upon short bursts of activity they are strong, but only for very limited periods of time.

Figure 5.14 Double Poling with a Stride.

Figure 5.15 Running Bumps: Make yourself heavy on the ski which slides downhill; light on that which goes uphill.

Running Bumps

All cross-country trails tend to have ups and downs and a good skier learns how to use these to improve on his forward momentum. Essentially the technique is to make yourself heavy on the snow when you are on a down-grade and lighten yourself when on an up-grade. You do this by trying to place one ski at a time on down-grades, build up speed, and then rise and skim over a small up-grade. If the trail crosses the fall line obliquely, one can also place one's skis so that they are always pointed downhill and keep picking them up one at a time as you slide along. This subtle placement and weighting of the skis on small down-grades is often enough to keep one moving rapidly forward and even negotiating small up-grades with simple inertia. Often, if you are sliding down a small bump, you can lunge forward and "ride" up quite a steep grade over a subsequent bump. It is good to pick one's skis up making pitter-pattering short steps quickly up the slope, thereby extending the effect of one's forward inertia by minimizing drag of the snow against your skis. I am a very effort-conscious skier and I enjoy running on undulating terrain where I can get these little "free rides". This makes the going much more interesting than, say, crossing a dead flat field or lake where only your muscles can preserve that precious forward inertia.

I find that there are numerous instances in our everyday life where we can capitalize on inertia and yet few people bother. A prime example I see whenever I ride on the subway. As the train moves into a station most people get up from their seats at least half a minute sooner than they need to and struggle towards the door holding on to the seats, etc. to prevent themselves being flung forward as the train is braked. They then wait, bracing themselves by the doors, until they open. If they had waited a few seconds longer, they could have used the last seconds of braking inertia to assist them from their seats and could have walked easily to the door and off the train while it was stationary. But they never do — nobody waits that long. I guess for fear they may not be able to get off in time before others enter or the door closes. It is an interesting study. Naturally, I enjoy using the trains' inertia to the hilt!

Figure 5.16 Skating: Lunge from one ski to the other kicking hard on each thrust. The skier must get lower and take longer steps than the ice skater.

73

Skating

Skating on skis is dead easy when the snow is firm and fast. Cross-country skis are so light that it is much easier than on alpine skis. The best way to learn is to try it on a very slight down grade. Out on a lake with a very strong tail wind it is also very easy. The trick is to stay totally relaxed while constantly shifting one's weight from one ski to the other with a good sharp push each time.

An ice skater can place one foot over the other while making a turn. On skis one can only allow more glide on one ski than the other to accomplish the same thing. Taking quick skating steps in one direction you will find that you can turn remarkably precisely. Skating turns on the flat are excellent practice for learning the step around turn when descending a hill (see page 78). Stepping around is a fundamental part of ski touring in that you are able to control your direction without any reduction in forward speed.

Learning to take big steps on the flat without losing your balance will increase your climbing speed considerably. I know skiers who can actually climb a hill in a flat traverse while constantly sliding downhill! They take very large steps uphill while keeping their skis angled slightly downhill.

CLIMBING

The longer you ski the less you will be concerned about climbing hills. I've known many beginning skiers who are reluctant to telemark down a long powder slope only because they know they will have to climb all the way back up to continue on the trail. The more you ski, and the faster and better you get at climbing, the less this will slow you down. Learning to climb swiftly will give you a chance for more runs than your slower companions.

Figure 5.17 Good technique on the flat is a pre-requisite for long distance touring or skiing with speed.

The easiest way, and almost always the fastest way to climb is to choose a route which minimizes the hill or enables you to keep a fast pace. Occasionally on very short steep hills it may be faster to make a straight-up attack if you have some momentum going for you already; but generally it's better to make a series of traverses away from the fall line. By zig-zagging in this fashion you determine your own gradient so that you can keep up a reasonable pace. I like to search out the undulations in the slope and follow them in a wavy traverse which never changes in steepness. When breaking trail in deep snow you will find that you can take a steeper line than would be comfortable for your companions following in your trail. They will not have the same resistance to backslip which you have from the deep snow. It is a good idea, therefore, to make your traverses easier than they need be for those following.

If the slope is narrow and not long, a faster variation on normal traversing is to use a modified side step (see Figure 5.6). This procedure allows you to adopt a much steeper line, gaining elevation more rapidly. It is much faster than a direct side step (see Figure 5.21). At the edge of the slope, or when desired, reverse direction either with a kick turn or directly by swinging the uphill ski around and starting off in the opposite direction (see Figure 5.23). This form of traversing often enables you to break out a trail along your intended descent path if the snow has a crust, or is extremely wet and heavy, making it difficult to manage.

Rapid traversing is one of the incredible advantages skis offer over any other means of travel on the snow. An extremely fast level traverse of a slope can be made by angling the downhill ski downwards and continually stepping up with the uphill ski to preserve your elevation. In the mountains if you find you must cross a slope with exposure to avalanche hazard you can do it in this way minimizing the time in which you are exposed and with little loss in altitude.

If the gradient of your traverse is flat enough you can keep up a diagonal stride gradually shortening the pace or length of stride as the hill steepens. Once your stride has deteriorated to a walk one should reach out with the forward knee to take in as much hill as possible on each step (see Figure 5.19).

Figure 5.18 Climbing on skis cannot be all physical struggle. You must use your head to find the easiest route.

Figure 5.19 When climbing, the skier shortens his stride in order to maintain his glide and appears to crouch somewhat lower on his skis because of the limited extension on each stride.

Figure 5.21 Direct Sidestep is useful where the slope is too narrow to Traverse.

Figure 5.20 The Modified Sidestep is a means to climbing a steep traverse line. It is much faster and easier than a Direct Sidestep.

Figure 5.22 The Herringbone becomes wider as the hill becomes steeper. A very tiring and often slow way to climb a hill.

The herringbone is familiar to most people and is without a doubt the most tiring way to climb a hill. Racers sometimes run small short hills effectively in this way and it is often the only way to handle a hill on a very narrow trail if you are not equipped for travelling off the trail. I invariably resort to a side step rather than herringbone because it is so uncomfortable. Sometimes it is just as fast as herringboning. In deep soft snow a direct side step can be awkward for each time you reach out with the uphill ski you bring down piles of snow on the downhill ski. Herringboning in such conditions is out of the question. The best solution is to use the modified side step, traversing as you climb, so that at least a portion of your ski is always falling in undisturbed snow at each step.

Obviously, waxing properly is important in hill climbing. Good wax with a strong bite makes possible much steeper angles for your traverses. However, even with severe backslip any hill can be climbed simply by thinking about the way in which you place your skis on the slope. Avoid steep angles of attack which will test the "bite" of your wax. Edging one's skis into the hill will help in preventing backslip.

Figure 5.23 Changing direction while Traversing must be done neatly and efficiently without breaking your pace.

The way in which weight is transferred to each ski is also instrumental in preventing backslip. I often find that firmly pressing the ski into the snow, not with a loud slap, but with a very positive and sudden weighting of the ski, and then a gradual transfer of weight first to the heel of the forward boot and then the toe, the ski will stay in position. If you place your weight on the ski in a jerky or erratic fashion it invariably will slip back no matter how good a bite your wax is providing.

If your wax is excessively hard for the snow you should plant the ski more sharply; if it is excessively soft, slide it into place and weight it gradually, thus avoiding the accumulation of snow on the bottoms. The more experience you have, the easier climbing becomes even with a less than perfect wax job. I seem to always wax on the hard side to insure good glide and invariably have a lot of backslip in consequence. However, with the traversing techniques for climbing which I have outlined here I never have any trouble in getting to the top of the hill and there is where the real fun begins! In the next section I will outline how to descend through all that hard-won altitude.

DESCENDING

Many books and magazine articles on cross-country skiing actually say: "You can't come down hills on cross-country skis!" One article I read recently showed an instructor in Steamboat Springs, Colorado demonstrating that the way to stop on cross-country skis was to drag your poles in the snow between your legs! Actually, descending hills is extremely easy once you apply your mind to a few of the fundamental characteristics of touring equipment. The alpine skier may be perplexed at how he is going to handle the moguls with these sneakers and match sticks! In fact, downhill skiing on cross-country equipment is a totally different sensation than alpine skiing. Control is entirely through steering the skis not by power carving of turns and checks which rely so heavily on edge control and the rigid boots characteristic of alpine skiing.

When the cross-country skier adopts the typical position of the alpine parallel technique; feet together, knees bent, body erect, he has no fore and aft stability at all because his feet are connected to the skis only by hinges at the toes. He has little lateral stability as well since he has narrow, very flexible skis with flimsy boots. He cannot bite into the slope in any significant way. In spite of these problems there are some experts who can handle cross-country equipment in parallel technique very adequately. My hat is off to them! Personally, I prefer a downhill technique which recognizes the limitations of the equipment and responds to it. In the following pages I will outline manoeuvers which will, in most cases, not strain the equipment or the skier and will enable you to handle any terrain and any snow. Descending hills is the raison d'etre for skiing for me. I think if I lived in Kansas I would probably not ski at all.

Figure 5.24 Downhill or Alpine Technique on Cross-Country Skis. The notched heel and hold-down strap on this binding/boot combination makes parallel technique possible, although not easy. Numerous adaptations similar to this are available. However, I recommend learning to ski with techniques more compatible with lightweight boots and skis.

Many novices, however, find skiing downhill terrifying on touring equipment and their opportunities for variety in their skiing are incredibly reduced in consequence. I like to plan every tour to include a long descent at some point, and preferably one in unbroken snow. Since most downhill turning technique on cross-country skis does not involve checking one's speed, but often only increasing it, it is not necessary to search out very precipitous terrain. Even gradual hills can offer very exciting runs if conditions are fast. Very steep descents are easiest when the snow is deep. Unfortunately, maximum avalanche hazard conditions usually accompany such perfect skiing conditions.

Figure 5.25 Straight Running

The best way to begin learning to ski downhill is to start out on a very gradual slope. Unfortunately, many first time cross-country skiers encounter a steep slope on a very narrow trail as their *first* experience! A narrow steep slope on a packed trail is probably the most difficult challenge you can have on cross-country skis and should not be attempted until you have developed a fair degree of confidence.

So if you are a beginner, check out the trail with others and make sure in advance that you can handle all of it before starting out. I think the whole process of learning cross-country technique should start in open country on the flat and on a gradual hill. Setting out on an unknown trail your first day can bring unpleasant surprises.

So starting on a gradual slope, the first thing to learn is straight running or travelling straight down the fall line of the slope with confidence. Since your feet are attached to the skis with hinges you must do one of two things in order to achieve some fore and aft stability so that you don't sit down or pitch on to your face. You must either slide one foot ahead of the other so that your weight is distributed between two separate points on the ground; or you must sit back with your feet together and most of your weight on your heels so that to pitch forward your body must be first raised off your heels. The first is called the telemark position (Figure 5.27) and the second, the tuck or racing crouch position (Figure 5.26). If you simply stand up with

Figure 5.26 The "Tuck" or Racing Crouch. Slipping one ski slightly ahead of the other improves fore and aft stability immensely.

79

Figure 5.27 The Telemark Position.

your feet together you may be lucky but the first patch of sticky snow or the first bump is likely to put you on your face or on your rear. Every inch that you move one ski ahead of the other improves your stability. The full telemark position is not required for a gentle run down a gentle slope. One ski a foot or so ahead of the other is usually ample. In straight running lateral stability is achieved by a reasonably wide stance(7 inches to 8 inches or more between the skis is a good idea depending upon your sense of balance.)Your poles are a great aid in balancing as well. If you extend them from your body they in effect become like the balancing pole carried by a tightrope walker. As your balance improves you will be able to increasingly narrow your track. Lateral balance is the hardest skill to develop on cross-country skis and is a key part of the telemark turn.

When straight running, I like to alternate between left and right ski forward and a tuck position. Do not remain fixed in any one position too long as this will only get tiring and prevent you from remaining flexible and able to respond to changes in the snow or terrain. Be ready to recover from momentary loss of balance by sliding the skis further apart and dropping your weight lower. There is no substitute in any type of skiing for a low centre of gravity to achieve stability. The full telemark position (see Figure 5.48) offers maximum stability. I have run directly up on a pile of brush buried in the powder snow without falling. It is the position which a ski jumper adopts just as he hits the ground and when his chances of landing on his face or seat are greatest. This is the reason jumpers use cable bindings which allow the heel to lift. The stance or distance between the skis in the telemark position is totally variable depending on need. Only when one attempts the telemark turn does it, of necessity, narrow.

I recommend that the beginner practice straight running descents, alternating between left and right telemark position, until he is totally confident before attempting to learn any turn.

Falling

Since falls happen to everyone and especially beginners practicing descents for the first time, this is a good point at which to comment on how to fall and how to recover from a fall.

Falls generally are characterized by the skier sitting down, falling on his side, or pitching forward on his face (see Figure 5.29). Most of the time he has little choice in the matter but I like to anticipate a fall and know how to respond. For instance, if when skiing in dense woods I lose control, I will always try to sit down and keep my skis and feet between me and any trees.

Out in the open on a steep powder slope I don't worry about a head over heels forward fall at all, and in fact, often this produces less damage than falling to the side or sitting down. Tree stumps or rocks covered by the snow are an ever present hazard and it is wise not to rely on throwing yourself out recklessly into the soft snow as a means of slowing your descent!

At the point when you realize a fall is inevitable you should relax entirely and concentrate only on preventing your poles from impaling you. On a very steep firm snow field, you should raise your arms over your head and drag them in the snow trying to achieve some braking effect so that your skis will swing below your body enabling you to regain your feet. Before skiing in mountainous terrain where the slopes are extremely long and a spill could result in a long slide into dangerous areas such as rock piles, it is essential that you learn how to perform a self-arrest to stop yourself after a fall. Actually the number of times one will elect to ski a slope where these conditions prevail are extremely rare. I remember once as a 12-year-old visiting Mount

Figure 5.28 The jumper must adopt the Telemark immediately before landing to prevent himself from landing on his face.

Figure 5.29 Falling: (1) sitting down; (2) on your side; (3) on your face.

Figure 5.30 Peter Griffin with trouble ahead.

lot safer than it looked! He then showed me how to tramp out a trough in which to put on my skis and I had a great time after that! I always feel more secure on a steep slope with my skis on, than with them off. This is one of the problems inherent in climbing a hill on foot to ski down. Until you have made that first turn and feel in control, you always wonder if you are going to make it. If you had *climbed* on skis you never would have had this uncertainty. In any event slopes so steep that a self-arrest is required to save oneself are slopes which I do not advise skiing on — certainly not with touring equipment in any case.

Once you have fallen, the first thing to do is swing your feet so that they are downhill from you and therefore more under your body weight. At this point it is a simple matter to stand up. Often to get your skis into this position you will have to roll over on your back. It is not always necessary to remove your wrist straps to accomplish this. If you are able to do it without doing so, it is just another thing you won't have to put back on once on your feet. Never use your poles to push yourself back up on your feet. This is only tiring and most inefficient. It is also a good way to snap a cane pole (see Figure 5.31).

Washington in New Hampshire on an April week-end (with my old wooden skis, no steel edges, cable bindings, etc.) I climbed up a long snow field carrying my skis and eventually reached a point where I dared go no further. Looking down, I was awed by the length and steepness of the slope. I didn't dare even put my skis on for fear of losing them. The only thing I could think of

doing was to jam them into the snow and start crying. Pretty soon an Austrian fellow came along and asked what was the matter. When I told him I was too scared to put on my skis, he came up to me, plucked me away from my skis and pitched me down the hill 10 or 15 feet or more. I immediately came to rest, got up and wiped the snow off and had to agree with him that it was a

Figure 5.31 After a fall rotate your skis downhill, placing them below you where you can stand up on them. Do not attempt to push yourself up with your poles until your weight is over your skis.

Checking

Checking one's speed, or slowing down, on cross-country equipment is accomplished by steering a course which is progressively further and further from the fall line. When you are perpendicular to it or on the level, you will stop.

Check turns involving stemming of the ski such as in the snow plow, stem turn, or christiania turn, are not appropriate to the lightweight equipment. However, inevitably a beginning skier will find that they are the only ways to deal with excessive speed. The snow plow is especially useful on a steep, narrow packed trail and I confess to using it in these circumstances myself. However it is much more desirable to check your speed in some way which does not place stresses on the bindings or around the wooden edges of your skis. Snow plowing under icy conditions can ruin a pair of wooden skis in minutes. Even synthetic skis are not designed for heavy abrasion of the edges. My orienteering skis have a single steel edge on the inside of each ski protecting both skis in a snow plow and the downhill or weighted edge in a parallel turn. Fig. 5.33 (3) illustrates a close stance snowplow being used to initiate a turn. In very firm snow conditions this technique may become a necessity.

One method of checking speed while running downhill is a ski glissade. Using both poles, as a mountaineer would use his ice axe, the skier can brake his progress quite satisfactorily (see Figure 5.33). Be certain to grasp the poles firmly and very close to their baskets to prevent them from breaking.

A

B

Figure 5.32 (A) The Snow Plow: Fundamental quick checking manoeuver, but one which is hard on cross-country ski equipment.
(B) The Ski Glissade: The key is to grasp the poles near their baskets and get low. An effective way to check speed on a narrow trail.

Figure 5.33 A variety of means for checking one's speed when turning is not possible; (1) (2) & (3) Early braking technique from single pole days; (4) One of the most effective Glissade techniques offering a measure of directional control.

Turning

Turns which control your path of descent with some precision are the best means of controlling your rate of speed. Subtle changes in direction are easily made in soft snow on cross-country skis simply by edging or tilting the ski in the desired direction. If you begin to descend a hill in a rather flat traverse it is easy to stop simply by leaning your skis uphill. Gradually your traverse will flatten until you come to a stop. I often use edge turns (see Figure 5.35) to avoid trees and other obstacles when running straight downhill.

Almost any hill can be easily negotiated by a series of very flat traverses terminated by an edge turn to a stop, followed by a kick turn (see page 66) and then the same thing in the opposite direction. If conditions are extremely difficult, e.g., glare ice, or hard frozen snow with no steerage, dense woods with brush on a steep slope, etc., this is exactly the technique I would use.

If conditions are a little better, e.g., breakable crust, or wind packed snow on an open slope, I use the jump turn (see Figure 5.36) which is handy for linking flat traverses since it can be done while still moving at a very slow speed.

Figure 5.34 Steered Turns used on cross-country skis have less checking effect enabling the skier to maintain good speed on less precipitous slopes.

Figure 5.35 Edge Turn: Subtle tilting of the skis initiates the turn. Very useful when straight running in the woods.

The jump turn is most exciting to do on a very steep slope as, while air-borne, you can drop a considerable distance (see Figure 5.37). If you're trying to lose altitude safely this can be an excellent way of doing it. Most people fall on their faces when they first try it. The key is to jump exactly when your ski tips pass your planted poles and to push off, once airborne, directly down the slope landing in an erect position with your skis perpendicular to the fall line.

Figure 5.36 The Jump Turn is much easier than it looks. It is especially useful in breakable crust and is actually easier to execute on a steep slope.

85

Well executed as in Figure 5.38 the step turn is quite lovely to watch. Note the low position of this skier as he literally springs around the corner.

You must develop an instinctive ability to be "light on your feet", flicking your skis away from a bit of shrubbery here, or a sapling there at the last minute, if you are to really enjoy skiing in the woods.

Figure 5.37 A superb Jump Turn on the Headwall at Tuckerman's Ravine, Mount Washington. While the extreme exposure of the slopes here demand Alpine techniques this is one manoeuver which can be performed equally well on either Nordic or Alpine Equipment.

Step Turning is perhaps the most common turn to make on cross-country skis. As learned on the flat (page 68) the change in direction is accomplished simply by picking one ski up at a time and moving it a bit at a time until you are headed in the direction you wish to go.

One generally picks up speed in a step turn due to the skating effect as you push off from one ski onto the other. Since most novice skiers usually are turning in order to slow down, they often get into trouble after stepping around something, speeding up, losing control, and sitting down. For this reason I recommend learning the step turn on an easy slope and gradually working up so that you can actually do it on a steep hill. It is a very quick means of changing direction if you find yourself headed for a big tree.

Figure 5.38 The Step Turn is perhaps the most useful cross-country turn, since it is very quick. Due to its skating effect, the Step Turn invariably results in an increase in speed.

The Telemark

By far the most useful steering turn on cross-country equipment is the telemark. It is the principal means for turning on cross-country or touring skis when travelling downhill in snow which is soft enough to have some steerage. One would not contemplate using the telemark in conditions where the snow surface was hard ice, heavy breakable crust, or thick wind slabbed snow. Other techniques descibed above are more suitable for negotiating these conditions. However, very heavy deep powder brings the telemark into its own. No other manoeuver on skis offers the complete control under these conditions that the telemark does. Alpine skiers skiing in similar conditions must rely on high speed and a planing action of their skis near the surface to control their direction and rate of descent. The telemark enables one to knife through deep snow with great precision.

Learning to telemark is frustrating for many people, since it is quite analogous to learning to ride a bicycle. The problem of lateral balance seems insurmountable, then suddenly, it becomes second nature. The process can be greatly speeded up if one progresses from step to step mastering each one before moving on to the next. I would suggest steps as follows:

1. Practice the telemark position standing on flat ground without moving, skis approximately 7 inches apart. Practice moving from the left ski forward position to the right ski forward position. The illustration indicates the optimum position which is one in which the forward leg is bent at the knee in a right angle, the shin going perpendicular to the ski.

Figure 5.39 The Telemark Swing.

Figure 5.40 Step One; Practice the Telemark Position in place.

The upper body is kept erect, also perpendicular to the ski, the weight is distributed uniformly between the skis and the arms kept low and extended outwards to provide maximum lateral stability. Practice switching from one position to the other, smoothly and rhythmically without losing your balance. Do it first with no poles, then with your poles, and finally with no poles and your arms crossed behind your back! The position often seems uncomfortable at first, only after you have done it for some time does it become more comfortable. Standing on the flat snow in the telemark position feels very awkward. I cannot hold the position for long. But the sense of awkwardness disappears as soon as one is placed in the position moving downhill rapidly, when it will seem much more secure than standing erect.

Figure 5.41 Stop Telemarks left and right after straight running.

Figure 5.42 The Telemark Turn.

<hr>

Five Steps to Mastering the Telemark

1. *Practice alternating right and left positions standing in place until you can do twenty smoothly without losing your balance (see Figure 5.40).*
2. *Repeat this procedure while straight running on a gradual hill.*
3. *Do the same with Stop Telemarks to each side at the bottom (see Figure 5.41).*
4. *Perform Stop Telemarks left and right on progressively steeper slopes turning away from the Fall Line.*
5. *Finally, move to Downhill Telemark Turns turning towards the Fall Line. Start with minimal Wedeln type swings on a gradual slope, not actually completing one before beginning the next. Gradually you will be able to advance to steeper slopes and deeper turns.*

<hr>

Figure 5.43

2. Now move to a gradual hill with 2 to 3 inches of soft powder on a firm base and practice these same alternating telemark positions while straight running down the hill, developing the same smoothness that you achieved on the flat. This should seem quite easy since in the straight running position, the skis can be kept 7 inches apart and lateral stability is less of a problem. After you are entirely confident in getting into the telemark position you have already progressed a long way in learning how to descend hills. It should be an instinctive reaction to sink into a telemark whenever uncertain of the terrain ahead.

3. The third exercise is to run straight down the same gradual hill assuming a telemark position, and on the flat at the base of the hill, make a turn to a stop in the opposite direction from your forward ski. The turn is initiated by tilting or slightly twisting the forward ski in the direction you wish to go. If you wish to turn to the right your left ski should be forward; if you want to turn to the left your right ski should be forward. A small amount of effort will initiate the turn. If the snow conditions are deep powder it may be

Figure 5.44 A Stop Telemark to the right.

89

necessary to shift some of your weight to the rear ski slightly unweighting the forward ski and making the turn easier to initiate. As the forward ski moves in the desired direction, the trailing ski should slide into the same track, its tip nestling against the forward boot. You will lean slightly into the turn as if riding a bicycle to maintain your balance and offset the centrifugal force which must be resisted to carry your weight around the corner. If you can manage six telemark turns without falling in each direction you are ready to try them on a hill. Don't attempt them on a hill until you can do them on the flat in the manner described. Don't be afraid to take some speed. Many people start out trying to telemark assuming the position immediately after they start moving and creeping down the hill. Some momentum is necessary, especially if the snow is at all deep, to accomplish the turn. So make sure you start out aggressively, poling to get started, and have sufficient speed when it comes to making the turn.

4. Having accomplished the above you should now try the same thing on the slope turning away from the fall line to come to a stop on the side of the hill. This is basically the same except that the opportunity for losing one's balance is greater. It is a temptation at first to lean into the hill and fall against it. In trying to overcome this you may find that you fall down the hill. It must be practiced coming to a complete stop in both directions. Each time you try, do it in the opposite direction so that you don't develop a propensity for turning in only one direction.

Figure 5.45 Telemark Problems: personally, I prefer to keep my hands low because I feel that the high position detracts from the appearance of the Telemark.

Balancing problems are greatly increased if you don't stay low.

All of the above manoeuvers should be attempted at first without poles so that use of the poles for balance does not become a critical part of your ability to accomplish the turn. First, simply extend the arms for balance and then when you feel you have it mastered, try clasping your hands behind your back in each of these manoeuvers.

5. Now you are ready for downhill telemarks where you turn from a traverse towards and across the fall line. When you can do this in both directions, actually linking your turn, you can really claim to have mastered the telemark. When turning toward the fall line your balance must be perfect. The lean to the inside is trickier because you must lean directly down the hill to initiate the turn *and* maintain your balance as you come around. It is easy to fall either to the inside or to the outside of the turn. Practiced on a gradual hill this really is not difficult. Only when you move to progressively steeper slopes does this balance problem become severe. Since you are moving from a traversing position towards the fall line, the rate at which you turn can make a great deal of difference in how difficult it is to maintain balance. I like to start beginners *only* initiating the turn in one direction and then immediately reversing the position and initiating it to the other side. Gradually one can deepen the swings from this wedeln, or fish-tailing approach, as the slope gets steeper.

On very steep slopes I drop my telemark stance much lower, my trailing knee often dragging in the snow. This often results in my rear ski crossing behind the boot of the forward ski, causing a spill. You must develop a sense of exactly how far you can go in dropping your centre of gravity

Figure 5.46 *The steeper the slope the lower the position.*

Figure 5.47 *With adequate balance the Telemark can be remarkably abrupt and a powerful checking manoeuver as well.*

close to the snow. I think perhaps the most important thing to remember is to get out over your forward ski if the slope is extremely steep and actually reach for the fall line. Extend the downhill arm out and twist the upper body in the direction of the turn. The steeper the slope, the easier it is to initiate the turn, the forward ski travelling in the direction of the fall line by the application of the slightest twist of the forward foot. Here the whole problem is balance. Once the turn is initiated and you are travelling on the opposite traverse, immediately switch to the opposite telemark position ready for the next turn. Do not carry across the slope with the downhill ski in the forward position since often it will be hard to prevent the swing from carrying you around to a complete stop. In very deep snow, or where the slope has a gentle gradient, it is necessary to make your telemarks in complete swings to avoid losing too much speed. The telemark is a steered turn and as such the ski never travels laterally through the snow. Therefore the skier's speed is diminished only by the fact that he travels a longer route than the fall line and therefore travels on a less steep gradient. Often one's speed actually increases in the turn as you are turning toward the fall line and assuming a steeper line on the slope.

If you find the telemark difficult, take heart in the fact that very few people today know how to do it all. It actually isn't that difficult if you'll practice each of the steps outlined above, progressing through them in a methodical way. When you can accomplish all of them even without poles and with your hands clasped behind your back

Figure 5.48 Superb Form: The weight is equally distributed on the skis.

Figure 5.49 The Telemark seen from behind.

you will have discovered a whole new dimension to skiing which, in my judgement, is the most exciting.

We have always taken great pleasure in decorating the hills with our telemark tracks. With ingenuity you can completely cover a field with a lace work pattern of inter-twining tracks, each one-ski width wide. It is not essential to have deep powder

snow to telemark, any snow which has some loose material on the surface is quite appropriate. Telemarks in corn snow in the spring are some of the best. Under these conditions one's speed is greater, of course, and it is sometimes difficult to avoid a slight stemming effect when the turn is initiated sharply in order to check one's speed.

Telemarks in the Woods

Telemarks in the woods are a great thrill in that one has complete control over direction so long as one is not changing the pattern of telemarks in order to retain balance. If you have mastered the telemark and your balance has become second nature, then you can basically steer in any direction you want to go with absolute precision. When skiing in woods the first thing that you will notice is that you are unable to extend your poles and arms out for balance because of obstructions. This makes it extremely important that you are able to telemark with "your hands behind your back". Skiing around trees is always dangerous and one must anticipate the beginning of the turn in sufficient time to allow it to happen where you want it to, and not a critical yard further down the hill!

I always have the feeling that if a truly athletic skier, like a Stein Erickson or a Guy Perillat (the most beautiful skiers I've seen) were to learn to telemark, they would do things still undreamed of with it.

Figure 5.50 Telemarks in the woods. The Author's father (at 80 years) in flawless form.

The Double Telemark

All of the telemark manoeuvers described in the preceeding pages can be accomplished with two or more people linking arms and moving together. As in "cracking the whip" on skates the person on the outside of the turn must travel faster than the one on the inside of the turn. In fairly deep snow on not too steep a hill this is really no problem at all and the two skiers will create absolutely parallel tracks over the full length of the hill. Sometimes helping a beginner in the telemark by actually skiing with them in this manner works quite well. There are very few manoeuvers in skiing that can actually be performed *with* another person, and the telemark is a delightful one.

Figure 5.51 The Double Telemark.

Figure 5.52 Unfasten your wrist straps when "Bushwacking" to avoid a wrenched shoulder.

Bushwacking

The art of skiing in woods is known as bushwacking and it is a great application for all cross-country technique. Sometimes it gets a bit hard on your equipment, your clothes and even your body. It can be dangerous if you don't build up your confidence by moving *gradually* from open slopes to dense woods. An apple orchard or maple "sugar bush" where the trees are well spaced and where there is no brush, is a good place to start. Practice all of your technique here before moving into denser woods or woods where there is brush.

Underbrush is the nemesis of the skier. It is really hard to avoid in most country. Europe is covered with forests where the ground has been carefully manicured between the trees, but paradoxically very few people there ski in the woods off the trail.

When skiing in country where there is much brush or many closely spaced trees it is wise to remove one's pole wrist straps since catching a basket in a snag can result in a severely wrenched shoulder. Wear close fitting tight clothing to minimize the chances of it catching on branches. Wear goggles to protect your eyes. I use downhill type goggles since light sun glasses used for cross-country skiing in open country will get swept from your head in no time. You must be prepared to plow into a soft pine tree or dense brush at any time. I know bushwackers who can ski directly down steep hills, crashing through the brush all the way, emerging unscathed at the bottom. All of us true masochists love to do it!

Figure 5.53 Jumping a Fence: So much fun it is worth looking around to find them!

OBSTACLES

Getting over or around obstacles is a most important part of ski technique if you like to ski off the trail, as I do. Unlike the snowmobiler who carries his trusty bolt cutters and enrages farmers by cutting fences, the cross-country skier can jump clear of most fences without even touching the wires and with very little delay.

Fence Jumping (see Figure 5.53) is extremely easy to do. Practice on a small wooden fence at first where you will not tear your clothing if you mess it up. Most important is that your poles are firmly planted on solid ground so that when you jump up and put your weight on them

they don't sink further into the snow leaving you short on altitude. Even if you fail to clear at the first go, it is often possible to teeter on the wire, move your poles to the other side, and hop down safely.

Figure 5.54 Tim Griffin clears a 5' fence.

Fence or wall rolling, (see Figure 5.55) is even easier than fence jumping although it necessitates removing a rucksack and sometimes involves getting a bit of snow down your neck. Make sure that when your skis land on the opposite side of the wall they land flat and not partially against the wall. This is a very easy way to snap off the tails of your skis.

A *Kick Turn* can be done over a low fence very easily (see Figure 5-56). Somehow kicking the ski to the vertical position makes it easier to rotate over the fence than simply trying to lift it vertically over.

Figure 5.56 Kick Turn over a fence

Figure 5.55 Fence or Wall Rolling caught by the high-speed camera. The entire manoeuver requires about 2 seconds.

Figure 5.57 Stream Crossing: Strong poles make it easier.

Stream crossings are commonly necessary. Skiing across ice is relatively safe since your weight is well distributed, but it is wise to test the ice first. Falling on the ice over deep water could be very serious, as your weight might go through and leave you hanging upside down on your skis! I prefer to ski rapidly across ice if I am to rely on it, so that I have enough inertia to carry me all the way across in one motion. Most streams are in gullies and it is necessary to traverse down one bank to the edge of the ice, do a kick turn, ski rapidly across and traverse up the opposite side in a

downstream direction. If the ice is slushy or there is open water, you can attempt to jump across using your poles, accepting the risk of wet feet. If the weather is cold and you get your skis wet they will ice up at once making it necessary to scrape them with a knife before travelling further. When skiing on snow covered ice, avoid dark patches. These may be areas where the weight of the snow has caused the ice to settle and water has seeped through a crack, saturating the snow. This slushy mixture will cake your skis instantly and freeze solid.

When you must cross a bare highway or road, pick your skis up in high careful steps, putting them down gently so as not to grind the gravel on the pavement into their bottoms. I never remove my skis to cross a highway unless it is covered with salty slush. In fact, I remove my skis as seldom as possible when out on a tour. After all, when one is skiing one should be able to ski over any obstacle!

Figure 5.58 First heat of a Relay Race . . . an all out sprint.

RACING TECHNIQUES

I said that competition was beyond the scope of this book and I really meant it. Modern racers are conditioned so much better than they were in the past that performances have continued to improve. The higher track speeds which are now being attained have brought many subtle changes to running technique. The diagonal stride has moved from emphasizing a straight and leaning body over a bent knee thrust forward to a slightly curved and higher body over a straighter knee. As the track speed has increased, the balance point in each stride, or the point at which the ski begins to slow down, has moved further and further out in front of the gliding ski.

For the tour skier this point falls under the shovel of the ski itself. The point is that if the racer's body weight falls in behind this point the glide is greatly shortened. With this point actually in front of the gliding ski, the racer must get up higher over his forward ski. This has the effect of "bounding" on to a more or less straight leg, rather than penduluming onto a bent knee. The number of unproductive motions is further reduced and the track speed is greatly increased. The timing of kick and hip/knee thrust in the stride has been brought closer together to become an almost similtaneous action rather than a kick followed by glide which is typical for the tour skier.

Figure 5.59 Bill Koch, Silver Medallist from Innsbruck 1976, **exhibits** modern form.

Figure 5.60 Bill Koch prior to the start of the 1975 Nationals.

The new racing stride is a development based on detailed study of natural body physics, not a sophisticated "system" for going faster. The racer who is able to capitalize on natural animal motions in this way to achieve greater track speed has a distinct advantage. Much of the modern racer's ability to achieve these speeds is due to the superb double camber of the new racing skis (See Chapter Three). These skis obtain fantastic glide due to their very stiff positive camber mid-sections (it takes a very strong kick to get them to bite on the snow) and flexible negative cambered tip and tail ends which keep the ski tracking. The skier's weight is very uniformly distributed over the snow maximizing glide. Conventional touring skis have a more flexible positive camber over their whole length and sacrifice much glide for ease in obtaining a bite. Any skier should be careful in selecting his skis for racing making sure that his technique is just a little bit better than what his ski demands. If this is not the case he will become frustrated by the backslip, lack of glide, and resulting exhaustion.

Figure 5.61 Bill Koch in the "Tuck" position.

Developing good racing technique demands interaction with a competent coach who can see your mistakes and bad habits. It is becoming an even more sophisticated field as in all sport today. Unfortunately, with more and more participants in competition, many youngsters do not feel they have a chance, and are unwilling to put in the hours and effort which training demands. Hopefully, however, this will be less and less the case as the number of cross-country skiers continues to increase. We have a long way to go before cross-country racing becomes such a popular sport that every high school has a team! Only when this is the case will we have the depth of first-class runners to compete with the Scandinavians, East Germans and Russians.

Figure 5.62 Koch in an aggressive Step Turn. Note the low crouch position.

CHAPTER SIX
WAXING FOR CROSS-COUNTRY SKIING

Skiers have always found waxing to be not only a source of wonder, but often of frustration as well. Most beginners, therefore, have good reason to be mystified by the complications involved, and I suppose this is what has encouraged ski manufacturers to develop "waxless" skis. As long as the only skis available were made of wood, waxing was really only essential under difficult snow conditions, since wooden skis both glide and climb passably on ordinary dry snow. However, proper waxing can considerably improve both the climb and glide and thus contribute to the pleasure of ski touring. On the new plastic skis, which are rapidly taking over the market, waxing is necessary at all times because without it, the skis backslip badly.

The tour skier usually encounters a wider variety of snow conditions than a racer who confines himself to a prepared track. While he may not demand as much in the way of performance as a racer, the greater variety of conditions he may encounter may impose severe constraints.

To take the mystery out of waxing, it is necessary to understand the principles which lie behind its performance; in other words, to know why it works.

HOW WAXING WORKS

Simply stated, the wax on the bottom of a ski has enough softness so that when the ski is weighted and pressed against the snow the ice crystals which make up the snow actually make microscopic indentations in the wax's surface. These indentations prevent the ski from sliding. When the ski is unweighted, however, and physically moved across the snow surface, these indentations are smoothed out and the ski slides freely. Sliding friction between the waxed surface and the snow crystals develops enough heat to melt a microscopically thin water lubrication layer on the crystal's surface.

It is said that the ice beneath a skater's blade actually melts to make it slide. I believe that blades which have been deliberately chilled to a very low temperature will actually not slide on the ice.

To the new skier who has waxed correctly, this phenomenon will seem like a miracle. He can climb directly up a hill without slipping back, and slide down the other side with no sense of friction at all. However, if he has no wax or has waxed incorrectly, he may find himself slipping back when climbing, and ironically experience quite poor glide as he descends.

Figure 6.1 Don't let the vast assortments of waxes baffle you. Start with one brand covering the broadest range of conditions with the fewest waxes. Learn the effects of heavy and thin layers; rough and smooth.

THE AGING OF SNOW

The key to understanding how to wax successfully comes first, as I said, with grasping the physical principle, and secondly, with knowing how to match the softness of the wax to the hardness of the snow crystals.

Don't be intimidated by this task. As soon as you learn a bit about the life of a snow flake you will begin to recognize the age of snow, its coarseness and its moisture content, all of which determine the wax that must be used. Figure 6.2 illustrates the degeneration of the beautiful, symmetrical powder snow crystal from what one sees on Christmas cards, to the coarse, rough ice grain we know as corn snow. Once the snow flake lands on the ground, this aging process proceeds under the influence of sun, wind and moisture, and is greatly accelerated by warmer temperatures or rain. The aging process, which is called metamorphosis, is considerably slower where the air remains cold, and especially when protected from the sun. Among my favourite places to ski are hardwood forests where on a sunny day perhaps only 10% of the snow may be covered by shadows from the tree branches. This 10% is constantly moving as the sun changes position and gives the snow in between shadows little chance to decay before the next shadow arrives.

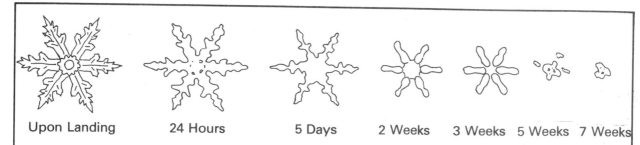

Upon Landing   24 Hours   5 Days   2 Weeks   3 Weeks   5 Weeks   7 Weeks

The larger and more rounded the crystal, the softer (or stickier) the wax required to obtain a bite. The bite, or climb, of a wax on dry snow depends not only on the penetration of the crystals in to the wax layer, but also on the adhesion of the snow to the wax. When the snow is wet, that is when there is a layer of water covering the surface crystals, this adhesion is non-existent and consequently, an even softer or stickier wax is needed to obtain a bite.

Figure 6.2 The Life Cycle of a Snow Crystal

Melting and re-freezing of the surface snow quickly builds up a structure, or crust, which thickens rapidly as melt water runs into the dry snow below. These conditions, if they involve a substantial temperature range, will convert powder snow to coarse granular corn snow in less than a week. On a glacier or high snow field, this corn snow gradually adds to the clear ice beneath it. Its melt water constantly saturates a thin layer immediately over the ice and then freezes. This process continues until only relatively firm ice remains in the summer. Where a snowfield is well drained this, of course, never happens, since the daily melt water from the corn snow runs off beneath and the snowfield gradually shrinks until it is no more.

Wind also hastens the aging process as it grinds and segregates the snow particles so that they form a dense, compact structure.

Another factor which affects the aging process of snow is the movement of the skiers themselves. As a track is formed and constantly used, the snow becomes more and more dense. At temperatures near freezing, the track surface may be converted to a continuous icy layer. Sometimes the first skier breaking trail is barely able to move while the next skier literally flies.

SCIA WAXING GUIDE

The proper wax for touring and cross-country skiing depends on the type of snow, how long it has settled on the ground and the moisture content. By selecting a number from each of the questions below, in sequence, you can identify a snow type. Waxes for that snow type are then listed in the table by manufacturer; only numbers corresponding to real snow types appear.

Is the surface...
1. Snow?
2. Ice, crust, corn or pellets?

Is it snowing or has it snowed in the last few days?
1. Yes!
2. No!

A handful of snow...
1. is very powdery.
2. blows easily.
3. blows with difficulty.
4. forms a loose clump.
5. balls up easily.
6. drips water when squeezed.
7. is a mixture of snow and water.
8. cannot be had.

EXAMPLE: 1 1 1

	BRAND			
SNOW TYPE	RODE	EX-ELIT	SWIX	REX
111	Dk Gn	Lt Gn	Lt Gn	Turqoise
112	Lt Gn	Green	Green	Lt Gn/Gn
113	Blue	Blue	Blue	Blue
114	Violet	Violet	Violet	Violet
115	Yellow	Tő Klis	Red Klis	Yellow
116	Red Klis Yel Klis	Tő Med Tjara K	Yel Klis	Red Klis
123	Lt Gn	Green	Green	Green
124	Blue	Blue	Blue	Blue
125	Violet	Violet	Violet	Violet
126	Red	Red	Red	Red
127	Red Klis	Tő Med Tjara K	Red Klis	Red Klis
226	Vio Klis	Tő Klis	Vio Klis	Vio Klis
227	Vio Klis Silv Kl	Tő Med Tjara K	Red Klis	Silver K
228	Blue Klis	Skare K	Blue Klis	Blue Klis

N.B. Type 124 is the most common!

Figure 6.3 SCIA Waxing Guide eliminates the need to know the air temperature.

The first skier does much more than create a track which offers less mechanical resistance to the second skier. He also physically transforms the snow into a water-laden ice, simply by passing over it. In dry, cold powder, the trail breaker creates a faster track for the second skier primarily by reducing the mechanical drag of soft snow. But, if a crowd of skiers moves over this track the soft snow will turn to ice.

The art of waxing, then, is simply matching the softness of the wax to the coarseness (age) of the snow. The SCIA waxing guide illustrated, (see Figure 6.3) simplifies wax selection by making evaluation of the snow easier. You do not even need to know the air temperature if you use this method. Most of the problems occur in *predicting* what the snow *will* be like once on the trail. Since most of my skiing is done off the trail this is much simpler for me. I find, in fact, that I seldom use more than 2 or 3 different waxes in the course of a whole season. If you ski on a trail however, you may find that a good variety is useful. If you race, you will undoubtedly find that each type put out by each manufacturer has its use. It is not a good idea to start out with a vast variety and with many brands. Try to learn how *one* manufacturer's waxes work for you, and keep using them. Waxing properly is a real delight, it's like making a perfect soufflé, it's fun.

BACKSLIP, BITE AND GLIDE

The phenomena of backslip, bite or kick, and glide are worth looking at closely. Waxing cannot prevent backslip if the camber and stiffness of the ski are such that the snow beneath is not adequately compressed along the whole length of the ski. I believe that roughly 4 grams per square centimeter are

Figure 6.4 The heel of the hand is better than a cork for smoothing out hard wax.

required to achieve good bite. Often a light person has difficulty in achieving this much pressure over a sufficient length of the ski. This, I believe, often accounts for children's difficulties in climbing hills. It is simple to figure out the average pressure under one ski for any specific skier, but a much more difficult task to determine the actual unit pressure for any portion of the ski. When confronted with a chronic backslip problem I often have swapped skis for a shorter, more flexible less cambered pair, and have seen the problem disappear even when both pairs of skis were waxed identically.

Large numbers of people to-day are buying very cheap skis which often have been stored improperly and have acquired excessive camber (not to mention warping and other problems!). It is sad that many will become discouraged and frustrated about waxing when the real problem lies with the skis themselves. Waxless skis are not immune to this problem either, but since most of them are made of fiberglass to begin with, excessive camber and stiffness are less frequent problems.

Good glide is essential both on level ground and when descending hills. Nothing is more frustrating than having slow skis. I would always opt for a bit of backslip in order to have good glide. The mark of a good cross-country wax is one that of course provides the greatest possible bite and at the same time gives the best possible glide. In choosing my wax, I would rather err on the hard side in waxing to minimize the chance of icing, which can completely ruin an outing. The hard paraffins used by ski jumpers and downhill racers are generally the fastest waxes for straight downhill running, but an appropriate climbing wax will yield virtually the same results.

One reason I resist the new waxless skis which achieve bite by means of mechanical deformations of the running surface, (e.g. fish scale patterns, or mohair strips) is that these surfaces cannot be as fast as a wholly smooth surface. The synthetic bottomed skis, on the other hand, are definitely faster than the normal wood bottomed skis.

PREPARING THE SKI FOR WAX – THE BASE

I almost feel ridiculous writing about the preparation of wooden skis for waxing, when to-day, fewer and fewer skiers are able to acquire them. However, I hope that somehow some of the smaller manufacturers will survive the competition from the synthetics and keep them available.

Wooden skis normally arrive from the factory with only a light lacquer protection on their bottoms. This should be lightly sanded away with fine sandpaper. The clean and dry bottom must then be protected by an application of grundvalla or pine tar sealant. This will prevent water from penetrating the pores of the wood, which would deform the ski and make the adhesion of wax impossible. The early skiers in

Scandinavia applied the hot tar only to seal the ski and protect it, they were not really concerned with waxes.

Many wooden skis being sold to-day have already had their soles impregnated with a coal tar derivative applied under tremendous pressure (resulting in a running surface similar to lignostone or compressed beechwood). Be certain that you have natural wood (hickory, beech, or birch) soles on your skis before attempting to apply grundvalla.

I use what I call the "torch and towel" method in applying the base. A small propane torch with a flared or spreader head (to produce a wide flame) is used in conjunction with an old terry cloth towel. First, place the skis bottoms up in a secure place indoors where they will not slip and slide around. Nailing a cleat to the floor to brace the tails and leaning the tips against a bench works quite well. Placing the skis upside down in a workbench vice is not so handy, since it is difficult to direct the torch onto the skis at this height.

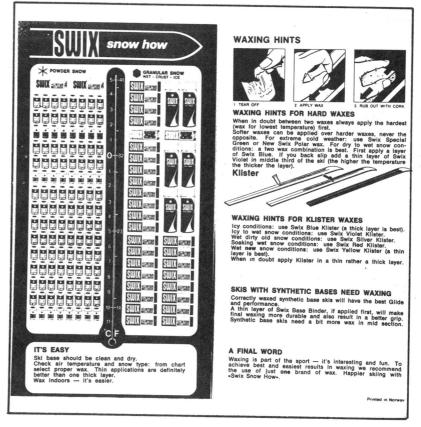

Figure 6.5 Swix Waxing Instructions. Extreme wax variety for the more sophisticated enthusiast.

The procedure is to first warm the ski by gradually sweeping the flame slowly from tip to tail, and by gradually decreasing the distance of the flame from the ski. When the ski is warm to the touch, apply the grundvalla (which should be at room temperature) dribbling it from the can down the length of the ski, or by spreading it on the ski with a flat stick. Usually a stream of about ³/₈ of an inch wide is enough. Next, spread this stream across the width of the ski with a bit of old towel, and immediately resume warming the ski over its entire length until the grundvalla begins to "boil" on the surface.

Then begin to clean, heating approximately 6 or 8 inches at a time and wiping it smooth. The grain of the wood will be readily apparent through the finished base. When finished, wipe off the grundvalla which has dripped on the sides and tops of the skis with a rag dampened in turpentine or varsol.

Try to avoid scorching the wood to the point of charring it with the torch. General darkening will do no damage. If the grundvalla flames up, simply wipe it off quickly!

This procedure is quite easily accomplished and normally lasts for some time. In localities where one skis only on powder snow one's base may last all season. If you frequent icy trails or worst of all, coarse crusty snow, it will quickly deteriorate. I patch the worn spots in my base every time I remove wax from my skis by using the torch. This, for me, is one of the great advantages of the wooden ski over any snythetic: it is so easy to remove old wax with the torch and towel method.

Make sure that the groove in the ski sole is perfectly smooth (with no lumps of grundvalla remaining). I usually run some fine sand paper down them once or twice after finishing the base, and then apply plain white paraffin to this area. I never apply running waxes into the

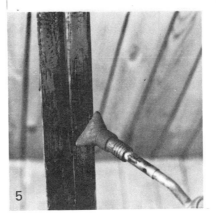
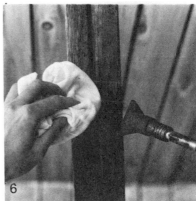

Figure 6.6 The "Torch and Towel" Method

groove, although some people do. The paraffin ensures that the groove will always be free sliding and never accumulate ice.

Coating the tops of the skis with white paraffin is also a good idea as it prevents snow from sticking on them and it protects the top finish. White paraffin available in a supermarket for canning jellies works quite well. Simply rub on a thick layer from the cake and smooth it down with the heel of your hand. If it lumps, a very light warming with torch will make it easy to smooth out. Silicone sprays are sometimes used for this purpose as well.

BASE WAXES

The grundvalla or pine tar base is an excellent running surface and holds waxes very well. Some people apply an additional binder or base wax before applying running waxes. Base wax, or grundvax, is something I've seldom bothered with, but it may be important to the purchaser of fiberglass skis. These depend far more on the adhesive quality of the wax to keep the wax on the skis.

Preparation of Fiberglass Skis with Synthetic Bottoms

The new plastic skis have bottom running surfaces of some combination of polyethylene or polypropylene (resins derived from petroleum). The nature of these materials is that they usually glide much better than wooden skis – especially on wet snow. However, without wax, they are very prone to backslip. Unfortunately, wax does not adhere very well to these surfaces without some special preparation. Fiberglass ski soles are therefore sanded in the factory to create a hairy, stringy surface to make possible a mechanical bond to the wax. The proper technique is to drip molten paraffin wax onto the ski surface and, by means of a blow torch with an ironing head attachment, or an electric iron set at low heat, smooth out the molten wax so that it can penetrate and saturate the hairy surface. When the surface cools and solidifies, a sharp, hard scraper is used to scrape off most of the wax, leaving a thin embedded layer. The operation should be repeated a second time for best results. Care should at all times be exercised to avoid melting the plastic sole. This procedure is analagous to the tar impregnation of a wooden ski. The skis are now ready for application of the running wax.

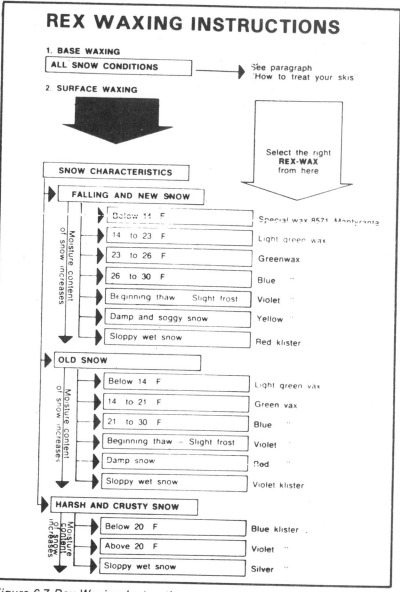

Figure 6.7 Rex Waxing Instructions

RUNNING WAXES

Running waxes are of two basic types – the "hard" waxes and the "sticky" waxes.

The "hard" waxes are all formulations containing large percentages of paraffin-type waxes along with other materials which modify the consistency. The "sticky" waxes contain little or no wax and are usually in liquid form and are called Klister. Klister is the Norwegian word for paste.

The hard waxes are used on dry snow and the sticky Klisters are used on wet snow — especially for abrasive conditions. The hard dry snow waxes are applied by rubbing it on the surface like a crayon. The liquid Klisters are applied by squeezing it out of tubes onto the ski surface and then smearing it out. One exception to this is the Jack Rabbit Klister, which is in the solid form and can be rubbed on like a hard wax. Most manufacturers make four or more "hard" waxes of varying consistency, so that the softer ones can be used in the difficult range of snow conditions near freezing. These soft "hard" waxes, however, don't take the place of the sticky Klisters, which have a much better bite on wet snow and much greater strength.

Application of all wax is much easier when the skis are warm and dry. Smoothing hard wax on to a wet ski is impossible, and smoothing soft wax on to a cold, but dry ski is difficult as well. I always apply a well smoothed out layer of the hardest wax which I anticipate needing first, and then apply a layer of softer wax locally under the feet to provide more bite if it seems necessary. I have already said a good deal at the beginning of this chapter about selecting the wax.

Figure 6.8 Klister is hard to smooth out unless heated with a torch. An exception to this is the Jack Rabbit Klister, which is "crayoned" on and smoothed out with a cork or fingertip – even outdoors.

The key rules are:
1. Carefully assess what the conditions are likely to be — anticipate weather changes, and whether you are to be skiing in or out of a track.
2. Apply a base layer of the hardest wax likely to be required.
3. Apply a softer wax for bite under the foot.
4. Stick to one manufacturer.
5. Learn to appreciate the effects of a thick or thin layer. The performance range is greatly enlarged by varying the thickness of application.

Generally, the older and coarser the snow, the softer the wax that is required. Figure 6.5 indicates the wax recommendations for one manufacturer, SWIX. The SCIA Waxing Guide on page (104) covers the RODE, EX-ELIT, SWIX, and REX brands. At best the ranges are very rough. Obviously, the trickiest conditions are those which span unusual combinations of conditions (e.g. dry, new snow and warm temperatures). Sometimes, I think that it is impossible to get more than 50% of the wax performance which one might expect. In very wet conditions it is most difficult to get good glide as the water-laden snow clings to the ski. Under these conditions melting the wax in a pot and brushing it on in "steps" is often necessary to break the suction between the ski and snow. This is the *one* condition where fish scale bottoms slide faster than smooth ones!

APPLYING HARD WAX

Hard waxes are rubbed on the ski directly from their tubes, and smoothed out with the palm of the hand or a cork. It is best to apply a number of thin layers rather than a single, thick one. A thin layer is easily smoothed while a thick one can wear out your hand! The friction heat between your hand and the ski will soften the wax. A finished thin layer will be fully transparent, and will only be visible by making a fingerprint. I like to keep my hard waxes relatively cool, so that when they are rubbed on the ski they go on like a wax crayon.

Figure 6.10 Simplified 2 Wax Systems: Swix "Skater", Toko "Touring", Jack Rabbit Johannsen. Of these simplified systems, only Jack Rabbit covers the full range of conditions that are otherwise handled by the "hard" waxes and the sticky klisters.

Temperature	Wax Applied	Wax Types			
		Johannsen Jack Rabbit	Holley Spray Cross-Country	Swix Starter	Toko Touring
40 F (4 C)	Rough	Wet	Wet	Silver	Plus
32 F (0 C)	Smooth				
	Rough				
20 F (−4 C)	Smooth	Dry	Dry	Gold	Minus
	Polished				
16 F (−9 C)					

Application procedures for the Simplified 2 Wax Systems.

Figure 6.9 Rex Scraper: Best for removing ice and hard wax from groove. Cork: For smoothing. Renofin: Wax remover for the hands

APPLYING LIQUID TYPE KLISTERS

Klisters of the liquid type which come in a squeeze tube should be reasonably warm when applied. About the consistency of cool honey is right. Because klisters are so sticky, it is best to heat them gently with the torch and smooth them out with a flat wooden applicator which is usually supplied. Try to keep the groove clear of klister. The most important thing to remember is to set the skis outside to cool completely before attempting to ski on the freshly applied klister.

While it is common practice to apply hard wax or klister to the whole length of a wooden ski, it has been found advantageous with plastic skis to limit the waxing to the centre section, under the foot. If backslip occurs, there are two possible expedients short of changing to another wax. One is to wax a little thicker and the other is to increase the area of the waxing.

MAINTAINING YOUR EQUIPMENT

I like to clean all soft waxes (klisters) from my skis after a tour unless I'm pretty certain I will need them the next day. Many solvents are available as wax removers, but I prefer to use the torch and a dry, clean towel. If I've worn the grundvalla base I often patch it at this time. In the spring it is a good idea to leave your skis in the hot sun, bottoms up. The tar will gradually work into the wood in this way.

Jack Rabbit "simplified" Waxing Instructions

In general, the Jack Rabbit Dry Snow Wax is used on all dry snow conditions, whether new or old, and at temperatures ranging from very cold up to the freezing point. If the snow is damp enough to cause backslip, then some of the Jack Rabbit Wet Snow Wax may be rubbed lightly over the centre portion of the ski, over the layer of Dry Snow Wax. Do not rub out.

If the snow is really wet, then the Wet Snow Wax is rubbed on in a thicker layer and smoothed out. The wetter and coarser the snow the thicker the layer should be.

Jack Rabbit Dry Snow Wax and Wet Snow Klister may be readily applied outdoors on the trail without the need of a torch.
Jack Rabbit Waxes work well on plastic and wooden running surfaces.

Figure 6.11

When cleaning plastic skis with a torch, be very careful not to melt the plastic. It is much better to use a solvent cleaner. After a first application, which softens the wax, scrape off the excess. The residue is then easily wiped off with a second application of cleaner.

Store waxes in a cool place. I recommend using a small fishing tackle box, big enough for your torch, old towels, grundvalla and assorted wax. One such chest per household is usually sufficient, but this usually means that one person ends up doing all the base maintenance. I feel that anyone who likes to ski should be prepared to spend the few moments it takes to keep one's ski soles well sealed and clean.

Figure 6.12 A little wax, even an imperfect choice imperfectly applied can make all the difference.

WAXING SIMPLIFIED?

I'm afraid all I've done in this chapter is make waxing sound more complicated. It just isn't. In recent years, since I've stopped racing, I hardly wax at all. In the deep snow off the track you usually find that a single hard wax will get you through the whole first part of the season, and when the snow turns to corn, one klister will do the job. Waxing is a very personal problem as everyone has different requirements. The point is it takes very little effort to achieve the rewards of waxing. I am very suspicious of the short-cut methods, spray-can waxes and spray-on base preparations, etc.

But I should not be listened to on these innovations, or on fish scale, or mohair strip skis, as I have very little experience with them. I *do* know that conventional waxing, using just a little bit of elbow grease, is easy and it really works!

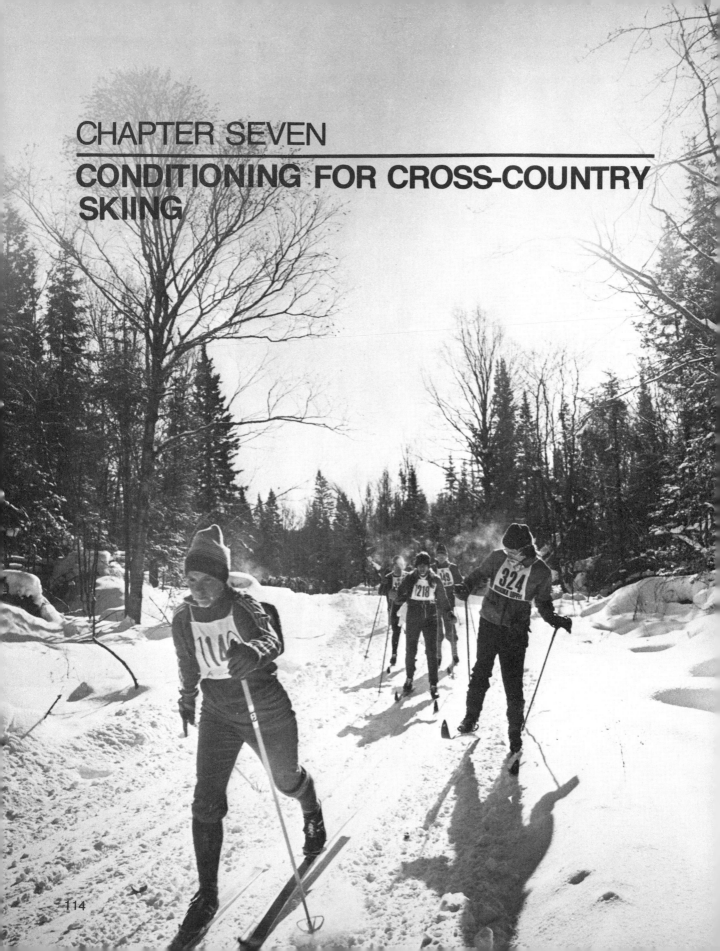

CHAPTER SEVEN
CONDITIONING FOR CROSS-COUNTRY SKIING

I like to think that anyone capable of enjoying cross-country skiing is already sensitive enough to look after their bodies throughout the year. Personally, since I've stopped competitive skiing I have given very little thought to conditioning in order to ski cross-country. Unlike alpine skiing where the unfit skier can easily lose control of a situation and get hurt, the unfit cross-country skier simply is unable to ski as far or as fast. I keep reasonably active throughout the year by running, playing squash and swimming and I simply look on cross-country skiing as part of an over-all desire to stay in reasonable shape. Cross-country skiing exercises a remarkable proportion of all body muscles. It subtly taxes our legs, arms, and shoulders on the level and while climbing, and gives us a rest while straining other muscles on the way down. It is periodical respite from an all-out strain which I have always enjoyed. It is unlike track and field events where you are pushed for every second of the way.

In this respect cross-country skiing is more like other strenuous activities (e.g. splitting fire wood, or shoveling snow) where there are intervals of rest as well as intervals of intense effort. Because of this most people find it tires them very effectively as they are lured into extending themselves more than they realize.

Figure 7.2 Few other forms of outdoor recreation keep you moving as consistently and for such extended periods of time as skiing.

Figure 7.3 Jim Galanes of Battleboro, Vermont, uses cycling for conditioning in the spring and early summer. Jim is a member of the U.S. Nordic Combined "A" Team. Later in the year he trains on roller skis.

CROSS-COUNTRY SKIING AS A CONDITIONER

The best way to train for cross-country skiing is, of course, to ski a lot. To gradually increase the duration and distance of your ski tours is the only way to prepare yourself for faster and longer tours. Training for cross-country racing is definitely beyond the scope of this book, however, it is worth noting that to train for a 50 km race it is necessary to run more than 50 km time and time again so that it becomes less and less of an ordeal each time.

There is no question that for people who are interested in adding a winter time activity to their year round program for keeping fit, cross-country skiing fills the bill. And we should all have year round programs to keep fit, shouldn't we?

Figure 7.4 Kayak paddling is a highly compatible off-season ski conditioner.

PRE-SEASON CONDITIONING FOR CROSS-COUNTRY SKIING

I spend a lot of the year bicycling and canoeing which I find very good for my skiing. Bicycling should be supplemented with running. Paddling a kayak on a river is a superb conditioner for the whole upper body. Many cross-country skiers are taking up this sport since it is so beautifully compatible with skiing and quite like it in many ways.

Bicycling has the same push and glide characteristics as skiing. It is important to allow time to insure that you are taxed. I ride approximately 40 minutes a day to and from work and that coupled with a very modest amount of running seems to keep my legs in shape for skiing.

Improving your cardiovascular capacity for skiing is much harder. At my age I am happy if I can preserve what I have. But younger people should test themselves through interval training to increase their pulse to its maximum then rest or slow down to allow it to reach approximately 120, then drive it to its maximum again. This procedure improves the body's ability to recover from strain quickly which in the course of skiing it is periodically called on to do.

Figure 7.5 Roller skiing simulates cross-country technique. Be careful on steep downgrades.

Roller skis for dry land diagonal stride training are quite good in that they do reproduce much of the same motion as actual skiing. Avoid steep descents on roller skis!

Running up hills with or without ski poles is a great conditioner for both cross-country and alpine skiing. It is hardly enjoyable, however. I much prefer a cross-country "thrash" through the woods or a swamp. This more accurately simulates a tour on skis for me.

Summer orienteering on foot is a great off season activity and certainly can give you plenty of exercise. You will find that your route decisions on foot are quite different than on skis. Traversing on skis, for example, is easy, but when running on only your feet it is always quicker to go straight down to the bottom of the hill and then cross to your destination.

I would urge those readers who are seriously interested in training for cross-country competition to refer to their national ski association to obtain team training recommendations and specific training programs.

CHAPTER EIGHT
SKI MOUNTAINEERING AND BACKPACKING

THE ART OF BACKPACKING

Carrying enough equipment to spend nights on the trail, or backpacking, is just as easy in the winter as in the summer. To the uninitiated this seems ridiculous but it is in fact true. The reason is that in mountainous terrain even in the summer one must carry adequate protection against very cold weather and this protection is usually close to being adequate even in the winter. The increased mobility which skis give you makes it often possible to carry fewer supplies than for a summer trip over the same route. In some areas weather in the winter months is equally, if not more, stable than in the summer, spring, or fall. Off-setting the extra warm clothing required in the winter is the absence of some items needed in the summer such as a tent rain fly. The weight of a camp stove needed in the winter usually is less than the wood cutting implements often carried in the summer.

If one dresses appropriately for skiing (see Chapter Four) one will find that the variety of clothing required in winter is no where near as large. I find that on summer trips I often end up with everything in my pack and wearing only shorts. I thus am forced to carry quite a large load. In the winter I find that I *wear* a larger proportion of what I bring and even with the warmer clothes that I require I end up *carrying* less. This is a good thing, because carrying heavy loads completely destroys the enjoyment of skiing for me.

Figure 8.2 Gerry Plastic Tubes are a tremendous way to carry any food of paste-like consistency. "Sandwiches" can be made simply by squeezing the contents onto crackers.

The true art of backpacking is refining your load more and more so that it becomes not only lighter, but also more compatible with your particular body and your actions on skis. Unfortunately, most of us take trips far too seldom to really learn from one trip to another. I constantly find myself carrying the same useless items trip after trip.

When your load is so light that you can ski all day in relative comfort and still be totally comfortable at night you will have truly discovered the art of backpacking.

Skiing into a wilderness area to establish a base camp from which you can make day trips, is, in my judgement, the best application for ski backpacking. A trip on which I must carry my pack for the entire time quite destroys the skiing for me.

Figure 8.1 Backpacking on skis enables one to reach remote and unspoiled areas.

EQUIPMENT REQUIRED FOR BACKPACKING

For a night or nights on the trail or in the mountains you will need certain essential items of equipment. On the following pages I will itemize the *minimum* equipment I carry on ski tours of various types:

Day Tours
For day tours below timberline in country I know extremely well and in very predictable weather I would take the following:

In a day pack:
1. Food for any meals planned on the trail
2. Emergency energy bar
3. Matches in waterproof case
4. Down "sweater" and anorak (if not wearing the latter)
5. Dry socks
6. Compass
7. Extra clothing if others in the party have not at least the same as I have
8. Trail wax kit (see Chapter Five) and spare ski tip.
9. Swiss Army Knife
10. First Aid Kit – toilet paper

For *Day Tours* above timberline or below in unpredictable weather I would supplement the above with the following:
1. Avalanche cord
2. Bivouac sack or plastic tube tent
3. Balaclava
4. Wind pants
5. Over-mittens or shells to replace skiing gloves
6. 10 hr candle, tin cup, several instant soups
7. Sun screening lotion (zinc oxide ointment, glacier cream, and lip salve)
8. Emergency goggles
9. Wax remover or torch

Overnight Trips
For *overnight* trips or day trips above timberline when the weather is unpredictable I would supplement all of the above with:
1. Tent with no fly but with frost liner
2. Cook stove and fuel, water pot
3. Sleeping bag with ground pad
4. Extra sweater, thermal underwear, or down "shirt"
5. Flashlight
6. Knife, fork and spoon, cup and plate.
7. Cagoule or rain gear depending on the season.
8. Sewing Kit.
9. Pre-packaged meals as required.

The first two types of trips can be accommodated in an ordinary day pack or summit pack. Only the addition of stove, fuel, tent and sleeping bag necessitates going to a larger pack. I highly recommend a form-fitting "soft" pack in lieu of a metal frame. While the latter are very versatile on summer trips for carrying large and awkward loads, the soft packs are much easier to ski with since the centre of gravity of the load is closer to that of the skier. Remember that a load of even as little as 25 lbs can make a great deal of difference to your skiing. First of all make sure your skis are adequately broad to give good flotation and glide. If you lose your balance a pack can prevent you regaining it. Make sure your pack is snug so it will not hit you on the back of the head if you fall forward. Look out as you duck under a tree branch, or you may not duck low enough for your pack.

If the route involves skiing in dangerous terrain where route finding is to be extremely important I would supplement the above items with:
1. Wands for marking the trail.
2. 2 Ice Screws.
3. 2 Prusik Slings.
4. 150 feet Climbing Rope 7 mm or 9 mm minimum diameter.
5. Chest Harness.
6. 2 Carabiners, plus 1 locking Carabiner.
7. Snow Shovel.
8. Snow Saw (optional)
9. Ice Axe (depending on nature of route).

Ski tripping without a tent, relying on the use of a snow saw, skis, and snow shovel to make a shelter can be a lot of fun. While your load is reduced by some 3 or 4 lbs (only) you must allocate several hours each day to build a proper shelter. It is an excellent solution if you are going into one area and plan day trips from a single base camp. Building an elaborate igloo or cave can occupy the whole first day and get you acclimatized for subsequent tours to higher ground.

To refine your load it is necessary to constantly review each item and assess its necessity. One tends to omit most toilet articles on winter trips since shaving and brushing teeth are so awkward. For a few days I think it is quite worth this small discomfort.

Often it is the optional accessories such as cameras, altimeters, binoculars, books and the like, that consistently increase the weight to be carried. I believe in minimizing these items. Bring a miniature super light camera such as the Minox, 35 EL, full frame 35 mm, fully automatic miniature model. I've never been able to read anyway as it is always dark by the time I get through pitching camp and cooking dinner.

FOOD AND CROSS-COUNTRY SKIING

Cross-country skiing makes many foods which would ordinarily repulse you, very edible indeed. When racing and near exhaustion a paper cup half full of warm tea mixed with a surgary fruit juice can seem like ambrosia. When your spirits are really sagging and your muscles seem sapped of the last ounce of effort a carbohydrate rich carob fudge bar or a pure dextrose tablet will pick you up so dramatically that you feel fresh energy within seconds. Of course a mile down the trail you've exhuasted this fuel and are ready for more! At the finish an orange, split open and eaten directly from the peel will never taste better.

On the recreational ski tour many foods taste quite good. Nuts and dried fruits, which at home tend to gather dust in the larder, on the trail are gobbled up in no time. In cold weather, one tends to "snack" at intervals rather than sprawling out for an extended lunch break. Conventional sandwiches made with butter or mayonnaise tend to be cold and clammy, generally not appetizing on the trail if it is cold. Far better are hunks of cheese, plain dry bread, very lean salami slices, crackers and the like. Dehydration is a tremendous problem of the outdoor winter diet.

Tips on Backpacking Foods

A man day of ski touring with a light load will require about 4000 calories and 75 gms of protein or more if weather conditions are severe and a great deal of climbing is involved. Efficiently chosen food for a weekend trip can be restricted to 2 to $2\frac{1}{2}$ lbs and 15 lbs or less for 7 days. Following is a table of caloric and protein values for assistance:

FOOD	CALORIES/OZ	GMS PROTEIN/OZ
Beans, dried	97	6.2
Macaroni or Spaghetti	100	3.6
Corn Meal	100	2.3
Oatmeal	110	4.0
Bread, whole wheat	73	2.6
Apricots, dried	86	1.5
Prunes & Raisins	84	.6
Potatoes, dried	100	1.2
Butter or Margarine	205	.2
Cheddar Cheese	110	6.7
Dry Skimmed Milk	100	9.9
Peanuts	168	7.5
Peanut Butter	173	7.3
Eggs, dried	166	13.5
Corned Beef, canned	76	4.2
Hard Candy & Sugar	111	0
Milk Chocolate	125	1.6

Figure 8.3

Oranges are an excellent way of getting moisture. On a normal day tour I often carry a vacuum bottle simply because the warm sweet tea or hot chocolate tastes so good! A bottle of wine is always welcome. I remember a Chilean Mateus that came in a beautiful compact round bottle which was easy to carry! Wine freezes in very cold or windy weather and can become quite disgusting. In warm weather cold beer is fabulous. Both wine, beer, and the vacuum bottle idea all have the disadvantage of having to be carried home. Obviously all are quite impractical on an overnight trip. Furthermore, alcoholic beverages should never be taken when there is a danger of becoming excessively cold.

Table of Specific Details for Stoves

	Weight Complete (oz.)	Weight w/fuel (oz.)	Dimensions Height (in.)	Width/diam. (in.)	Length (in.)	Fuel	Fuel Capacity (oz.)	Boiling Time [1] (min.)	Burning Time [2] at Simmer (min.)	Pressure Pump	Built-in Cleaner	Needs Priming Fuel	Cold Weather Usage	Simplicity
Primus Grasshopper	11.5	43.0	3¼	3¼	17	Propane	14.1	7	360	NA	NA	No	Maybe	High
Bleuet S-200	15.0	24.0	4½	3½	9½	Butane	6-1/3	5	210**	NA	NA	No	Poor to No	High
Gerry Mini Mark II	8.0	18.0	—	4½	1½	LP Gas	6¼	6	195	NA	NA	No	Maybe	High
Optimus 77A	24.0	—	4½	8	—	Alcohol	6	7½	25	NA	NA	No	Yes	High
Svea 123	17.5	22.0	5	4½	—	White Gas	6	6	60	No	No	No	Maybe [3]	Avg.
Optimus 8R	23.0	28.0	3¼	5	5	White Gas	3¼	7	55	No	Yes	No	Maybe [3]	Avg.
Phoebus 725	22.0	30.0	4½	5½	—	White Gas	10	7	105	No	Yes	No	Yes	Avg.
Phoebus 625	32.0	48.0	7¼	5½	—	White Gas	16	4½	190	Yes	Yes	No	Yes	Avg.
Optimus 111B/111	54.0	66.0	4	6¾	7	Wht. Gas/Kero.	16	6	110	Yes	Yes	No/Yes	Yes	Avg.
MSR 9	15.0	32.0*	3½	3¼	9¾	White Gas	16 or 32	4	130	Yes	No	No	Yes	Avg.

* with pint of fuel
** with jet gas

1. Boiling time is time it took to boil 1 quart of average temperature tap water. The stove was operated in a warm room. Times will vary greatly with altitude, air temperature and wind.
2. Burning time is total time stove can maintain a rolling boil in a quart of water. These times will increase if the stove is set to a light simmer, and decrease if the stove is opened to its maximum.
3. Stove will operate well in winter if the Optimus Mini-pump is added.

Figure 8.4 Stove Comparison Chart: MSR 9, Primus Grasshopper and Phoebus 625 all rank high depending on your requirements.

Overnight trips require hot food and the use of the camp stove, unless you are to travel in heavily forested areas, where ample firewood abounds. Even in these conditions I tend to like the stove which can be used either in the tent or at the door of the tent.

The advent of freeze-dried food technology has completely revolutionized back-packing foods so that menu planning and preparation are riduculously simple. The only problem with freeze dried foods is their cost. When budgeting for a trip you should figure the cost of each meal as equal to that charged by a good restaurant. Money can be saved by preparing your own food from simply transported items such as rice, oatmeal, dried soups, instant mashed potatoes and other semi-prepared foods easily found in a supermarket. Because of the dehydration problem a large proportion of your food intake will be in hot liquids such as soup, cocoa, or hot chocolate, and tea.

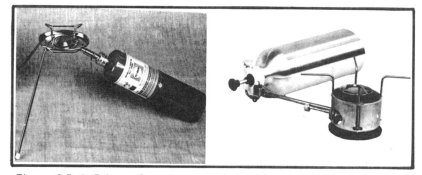

Figure 8.5 1. Primus Grasshopper: Perfect for short trips. Safe to use inside a tent. 2 lb. 11 oz. unit will burn 6 hours on a low flame. I calculate 6 meals per propane cylinder; 3 or 4 if melting snow for water is required. I always start a trip with a new cylinder and use my "left-overs" for waxing. 2. MSR 9: This stove is of superb design since it utilizes a fuel storage bottle as pressure reservoir. It has the same problems as any liquid fuel stove, but is a fantastic performer.

Main courses should consist of such semi-liquid items as boeuf bourgignon, chile con carne, or creamed chicken poured over rice or potatoes. I prefer to restrict a winter meal to one plate of food all capable of being served at once so that no items get cold waiting for another to be served.

One superb brand of beautifully prepared and seasoned freeze dried food is "Mountain House". All of their delicious meals are contained in plastic bags to which you simply add boiling water, wait 5 to 10 minutes and then eat. This has the great advantage of leaving no dishes to wash! I quite often do not bring a plate at all, but only a cup large enough to eat oatmeal from.

After oatmeal with brown sugar (try "instant" oatmeal made in the cup as well to avoid washing up) I then make a cup of tea or instant coffee which adequately cleans out the cup so that it can be wiped clean. Modern camping with these miracle foods is dead easy!

I list below the food I bring for 2 people spending two nights on the trail:

For lunches and snacks

4 oranges
2 boxes of crackers – (wrap separately)
$\frac{1}{2}$ – $\frac{3}{4}$ lbs of cheese
2 - 8 oz chocolate bars
1 tube jam or peanut butter
1 tube of paté
12 oz dried apricots, prunes, or raisins

For dinners and afterwards
2 freeze dried dinners for 2
6 individual packaged dried soups
8 tea bags
1 package crackers
2 freeze dried desserts or similar treat
2 chocolate bars

For breakfast
4 instant oatmeals
3 oz. brown sugar
4 tea bags or instant coffee
2 packages of dried fruit drink (e.g. "Tang")

Alternatively: freeze dried scrambled eggs or simply powdered egg plus bacon bits. In planning your food remember:

1. crackers weigh less than bread
2. paste-like foods should be carried in refillable plastic tubes
3. avoid anything that must be carried out such as tin cans and glass
4. plastic can be burned or melted in a fire — aluminum foil cannot
5. avoid washing up entirely if you can
6. Wrap everything separately in case some things get wet or smashed. This is good canoe trip advice but also is true when winter camping.
7. Divide the load so that if for some reason a pack is lost a reasonable balance of food is still available in other packs.
8. Take a little less than you think you will need. While I believe in having plenty to eat, and also being prepared for more days than I anticipate for the trip, once I've decided on the number of day's food I am to carry, I deliberately reduce quantities to a minimum. Nothing is worse than returning bloated from over-eating and carrying leftovers. Far better to come home slightly hungry. Home cooking will then taste that much better!

There are some ingenious foods that people have devised for eating on the trail. I include the following recipes.

Fruit Leather
Pieces of this can be used as an inner sole in your boots! It takes no space and yet will sustain you many days.

1. Smear fruit baby food $\frac{1}{4}$ inch thick over a cookie sheet.
2. Set in oven overnight at 150° degrees with oven door ajar.
3. Next day cut in strips and roll up in plastic wrap.

Mountain Bars
1 package (6 oz.) butterscotch chips
$\frac{1}{4}$ cup honey
$\frac{1}{4}$ cup raisins
$\frac{1}{4}$ cup flaked coconut
$\frac{1}{4}$ cut chopped walnuts
$\frac{1}{2}$ cup wheat germ
$\frac{1}{2}$ cup oatmeal
Melt butterscotch chips in saucepan, blend in honey, gradually add all other ingredients stirring until mixed. Place mixture in greased baking pan and allow to cool until eaten.

Crunch Balls
2 cups crunchy peanut butter
1 cup honey
3 cups oatmeal
$\frac{1}{4}$ tsp. vanilla
$\frac{1}{4}$ tsp. salt
$\frac{1}{2}$ cup crushed nuts.
Heat peanut butter and honey until slightly fluid. Sir in oatmeal, vanilla, salt, and nuts. When cool form into balls and wrap.

Paté from liver, anchovies, and a variety of other foods are sold in tubes. Mustard and certain jams are also sold in handy tubes. Corned beef removed from its tin is excellent after several days on the trail if carefully wrapped in plastic.

Figure 8.6 Phoebus 625 and 725: The 625 is "the old reliable" most favored among mountaineers. It always works regardless of cold or wet. It is heavy and can burn your tent down, but treated with respect, it will serve well. The 725 model has no pump and is not recommended.

Eating well under conditions where there are other living hardships or potential hardships is one of the great pleasures of life. In the summer, setting off in a canoe, I've often brought a complete steak dinner, corn on the cob, wine, buttered rolls . . . the works, for the first night. I don't recommend trying anything like this in the winter as complicated food to cook or eat will completely ruin the enjoyment of the meal. The key here is simplicity — getting fed while keeping warm and comfortable. As you gain experiences you will develop your own winter-time gourmet treats! You will discover that different food tastes better on a ski trip than it does at home. There are endless back-packing cook books on the market from which to get ideas. Figure 8.3 itemizes some important tips on backpacking foods.

Figure 8.7 Sigg Swiss-made aluminum cooking kettles and water/fuel bottles. The fuel containers are compatible with the MSR stove. The cook pots are superb. 1-2 qt. size is adequate for 2 people. The lid can be used as a fry pan if necessary. In the winter I try to use stove and pot only for boiling water so as to avoid any cleaning up.

On Eating Snow

Getting moisture into your body throughout the day when skiing is important on long trips. I always tell children never to eat snow as this can be dangerous if you actually swallow a piece. It can cause severe stomach cramps which will leave you in no condition to ski. However, if you are very careful you can melt small amounts in your mouth and then swallow the melted water. Be sure your food contains ample salt, or use salt tablets, as dehydration will rapidly lower your body salt level. On longer trips it is wise to bring and use a high potency, multi-vitamin mineral supplement as well.

A Word About Melting Snow and Stoves

Melting snow consumes a lot of heavy fuel. If at all possible try to find a campsite where you can collect water from a stream or dripping water fall. Fill a plastic bag during the sunny day for use later at night when these sources may no longer be running. You can build a water collector too to leave at your base camp producing water while you are off skiing during the day. Simply build a sloping snow wall facing south and angled at approximately the amount of latitude of your geographic position. Along the base of the wall cut a deep gutter sloping to a pit where you place your collecting pot wrapped in some clothing so as to insulate it from the snow. With experimentation you will find that you can collect far more water than you need in no time at all. All snow melt water is very dirty regardless of where you are (actually this may not be true in the high arctic but I have certainly found it so from Alaska to Peru). Plan on straining melt water through a handkerchief before bringing it to a boil. When pouring boiling water into someone's tea cup in the darkness, never pour the last few drops.

Chances are they are a horrible grey sludge. Melt water collected during the day and allowed to settle often is very clean near the top.

Stoves should be selected with great care and based on efficiency; that is the amount of water boiled per cc of fuel or total weight of stove and fuel. Most are quite reliable, almost all can blow up or burn your tent down if not used with care. Carry a cleaning and repair kit to clean clogged jets and replace worn pump leathers. Do not light the stove if it is covered with spilled fuel! Practice at home lighting it dozens of times under all conditions before attempting to cook with it on a trip. Practice lighting it when thoroughly wet and after having been left outside overnight. Be thoroughly familiar with your stove so that you can handle it in darkness.

For short trips of 1 or 2 nights a propane stove is great. The steel cylinder is heavy but not much more than a corresponding number of BTU's in a liquid fuel container. They light instantaneously so they are conveniently turned off in between courses, etc., thus conserving fuel. Estimating the fuel remaining so as to ration it is quite difficult so take no chances. Use a new cylinder and save your old ones for ski waxing at home!

Propane stoves, I think, are safe to use *in* a tent while I have never felt secure with any liquid fuel stove. The "Phoebus 625" is my favourite of the latter and I've had some frightening "flame-ups" with it. Nothing, I imagine, could quite compare with the misery and stupidity which one would feel having just burned one's tent down, high on a cold mountain. It is an experience I never want to have.

Avoid butane fired stoves and for that matter, butane fired waxing torches. When this fuel is very cold it simply will not burn with any intensity at all. It is not a pleasant task to have to warm the fuel with body heat as I have done simply to get it to burn!

Figure 8.8 A high quality winter camping tent is the Gerry "Himalayan".

TENTS, IGLOOS, AND OTHER SHELTERS

Nothing quite compares to being warm and snug in your sleeping bag after a strenuous day skiing if you are in a proper shelter. Principal problems to deal with in selecting a shelter are: (1) wind, (2) moisture, and (3) warmth.

Tents are very comfortable if the right circumstances are present. These are adequate means for pitching the tent: tent pins don't work in snow so either ski poles, sticks from trees, ice axes, ice screws, skis, snow shovels, or other devices must be used to anchor the ends of the tent. A tent designed for snow camping has three accessories which summer tents usually do not: snow flaps, a frost liner, and a cook hole. The first is an aid in pitching since snow can be shovelled on the flaps in lieu of using anchor pins. One danger with snow flaps is that they will freeze in, making the tent impossible to remove without damaging the flaps. The frost liner is an inner tent roof which is made of absorbent cotton. As exhaled breath and cooling moisture condenses it freezes on the liner. In the morning before breaking camp simply untie or unsnap the liner, gather it up carefully and shake it outside. All of the frost will fly off. I try hard to minimize internal moisture by cooking outside the door when practical as a layer of frost overhead is not too pleasant. A frost liner tends to make the tent a bit warmer as well. The third accessory, the cook hole, is a zippered opening in the floor of the tent where the stove and any hot pot can be placed on the snow if necessary. I've also known them to be useful in giving access to very deep pee holes in the snow!

Pitching a tent is far quicker than building any alternative snow shelter; hence their popularity. They also offer a nice dry floor on which to spread out. In heavy winds they all are less than comfortable although some designs, utilizing double curved surfaces are remarkably good. The external frame types, although a bit heavier, are quite good in the snow as they need little in the way of anchorage.

Figure 8.9 Two tents made by Snow Lion: The "Triplex" and in the foreground, the "Mountain" model.

When tenting in deep woods I used to like to put a layer of boughs beneath the tent to separate it from the snow. Unfortunately, this is only practical now in very remote wilderness areas. If it were to become common practice, our forests would quickly become denuded around every campsite!

Figure 8.10 External frame tents such as the "Oval Intention" made by North Face, are excellent for snow in that they are totally self-supporting.

Igloos and Other Snow Shelters
Igloos and snow caves are fabulous shelters offering maximum resistance against wind and cold. The famed arctic explorer, Vilhjalmur Stefansson, in the arctic in 1912, noticed that it could be 100°F (+40°C) warmer inside an igloo than outside. When it was –50°F (–45°C) outside he recorded temperatures of –40°F (–40°C) in the entranceway, 0°F (–17°C) at the door, +20°F (–6°C) at the floor level, 40°F (4°C) at shoulder height and sometimes a torrid 60°F (15°C) near the ceiling. Stefansson and others such as Perry were the first arctic explorers to really put the igloo to use. Constructing an igloo in a really exposed and windy location, exactly where one would normally *not* choose to camp, is a great thrill. Lionel Terray spent several days in an igloo on the very summit of Mount Blanc!

All that is needed to build an igloo is *deep* snow, a shovel and a snow saw. The snow saw is the only specialized tool required. Sometimes when conditions are perfect, it is possible to cut blocks with a ski or a small snow shovel. However, with a saw it is always possible. Figure 8.11 illustrates a good shovel and saw.

Igloo building is another thing you should experiment with at home before placing yourself in a position where you have to build one to survive. Building a proper one from shaped blocks takes an eskimo an hour or more, and you or I *after a lot of practice,* and when conditions are perfect, at least twice as long. It is wet work and it is wise to wear either rain gear or wind pants, a parka with hood drawn snugly, and rubber gloves over woollen mittens.

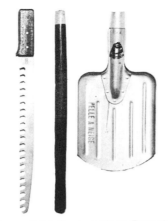

Figure 8.11 An excellent French snow shovel with a removable handle. It weighs 1 lb. 5 oz. The Blade is 7¹/₂ inches by 9¹/₂ inches. The snow saw pictured is the best one available. It is 20 inches long and weighs only 6 oz.

To saw snow blocks one needs firmly compacted snow. Wind slab snow is perfect. Often however the snow available is soft and it seems like a hopeless task. There is usually a means for compacting the snow though. The way to do it is first *with skis on,* tramp out an area about 2¹/₂ times as large as the house you intend to build. Then remove your skis and do it on foot, smoothing out the surface with a snow shovel. Now *get off the area* and allow it to set, undisturbed.

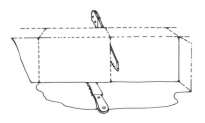

Block Cutting: Be Precise. Do Not Attempt to Lift Block Until It Falls Loose. Do Not Score Adjacent Blocks Causing Weak Points.

About ¹/₂ hour is required for a bond to develop between the newly compacted snow crystals. Any walking on the snow during this period will cause fracture planes throughout the snow which will show up as soon as the snow is cut into blocks. Use the time to dig a deep trench alongside one end of the area. This will give access to the snow blocks and be extended to form the entrance tunnel. Cut and stockpile blocks with the saw making certain that all faces are sawn. Work with precision so that the underlying snow layer does not become scarred, weakening subsequent blocks. Figure 8.12 illustrates the step by step formation of the igloo. Note the importance of insuring that when placed, each block bears on three points only; its two bottom corners and the upper corner in contact with the adjacent block. In this way diagonally crossing compressive stress lines develop in the snow to form a rigid (lamella) structure.

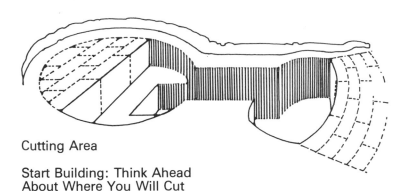

Cutting Area

Start Building: Think Ahead About Where You Will Cut Blocks

Build First Course and Pack Securely with Snow

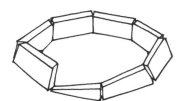

Cut Continuous Ramp Course So That All Succeeding Courses are Inclined

All Subsequent Blocks should Bear on Three Corners as They are Placed Enabling Them to Stand by Themselves.

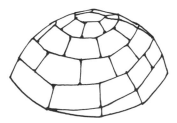

Run the Saw Through the Joints as Required to Insure Good 3 Point Contact Between Blocks.

Figure 8.12 Igloo Construction

After joint packing and consolidation the igloo becomes a monolithic dome of considerable strength. The slightly concave edges of each block that result from shaving to insure this good corner contact, leaves large cracks which should be packed with snow after the blocks are securely balanced in position. I prefer to wait until I have been around a full course before doing this chinking. Cutting the "ramp" into the first course makes it easy to start the next as the first block has something to lean its upper corner against. I remember as a child attempting to build igloos and desparately trying to *balance* the first snow block on each course. The only way to do it is to have about 8 people holding blocks until a final one can be placed!

While naturally quite dark if walls are kept thick, the igloo can be lit by a skylight or "window" made from a thin slab of ice which can be "custom frozen" to whatever shape you desire. A small vent should be cut in the roof and opened whenever a stove is used inside. It can be plugged with a mitten when not in use. Contrary to popular belief, carbon monoxide does not slide out the lower entrance tunnel as it is lighter than air.

Figure 8.14 Igloo living is comfortable! (Thor Jacobsen composing an epic)

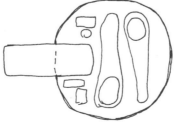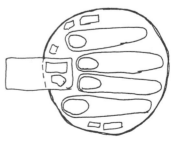

Figure 8.13 The Finished Igloo: Various Plans

Figure 8.15 "The Kitchen"

Usually one builds an igloo in areas where there is a high wind. This will erode the outer wall if one does not build a "snow fence" of snow blocks on the windward side. It is wise to place the entrance tunnel perpendicular to the wind direction so that it does not become clogged or drifted over. When finished an igloo may be "fired" for permanence by building a fire inside, closing the vent hole and covering the entrance. The fire heat melts the inside snow saturating the wall. When the igloo is re-opened and allowed to freeze, the resulting dome is incredibly tough and will often withstand major rainstorms and thaws afterwards. Normally, however, such lengths are not necessary as simple body and cooking heat will "set" an igloo quite satisfactorily.

Cutting and shaping a bed platform and steps into the tunnel is best done after the igloo is entirely complete and the "debris" has all been scraped out. Niches for candles can be carved as well as for food and gear. Figure 8.13 illustrates a few ways of "planning" an igloo. Remember that an igloo is virtually soundproof so don't try to call out to someone on the otherside of its walls. At night keep all of your gear and tools inside in case the winds change and you have to dig your way out.

Other Structures
Oftentimes, snow conditions, lack of implements, or weather will make construction of a full fledged igloo impractical. Once, I constructed an emergency snow cave with one other companion on a smooth, hard, windblown snow field at 21,000 feet on Mt. Huascaran in Peru in about 1 hour using only our ice axes. It was a very small hole (only one could chip at a time) and a most uncomfortable night was had by all; but it was shelter. We could see some small crevasses about 500 feet ahead which might have offered better shelter but rather than risk that much more walking before darkness fell I reasoned that we should concentrate on digging where we were. In the morning we passed those small crevasses and they didn't look very comfortable! A simple cave is the easiest type of shelter and one that can generally be carved even using only a ski, from firm snow. Adhere to good igloo principles: keep the space no larger than necessary; keep the entrance small and low and sheltered from the wind; cut a ventilation hole if you do any cooking. Figure 8.16 illustrates a few alternatives.

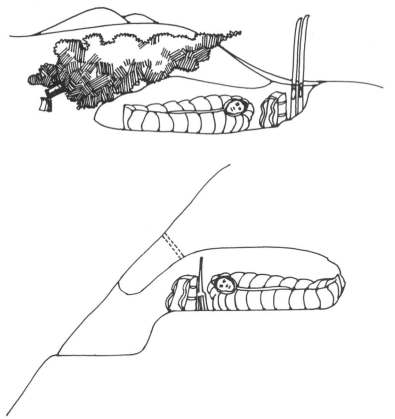

Figure 8.16 Alternative Snow Shelters

Sleeping with no Shelter

To spend a comfortable night in the open in the winter, staying warm and sleeping well, gives one a tremendous sense of satisfaction in overcoming a very alien environment. This is especially true when sleeping outdoors *without the aid of any shelter* where one's face is exposed to the open air throughout the night! One can see the stars in the sky, see the dawn light and hear all of the sounds of the night. With proper preparation it is possible to sleep without the aid of a tent or igloo outdoors in the winter far more easily than in the summer. The risk of rain is minimal and there are no insects. Winter precipitation is usually cold dry snow and far easier to contend with than rain. As long as one is dry the problem of staying warm is infinitely easier to solve.

The key pieces of equipment required to spend a comfortable night outdoors are: first, some form of insulation to place beneath the body, between the snow and the sleeping bag to reduce heat losses into the snow; secondly, a first rate quality sleeping bag made either of synthetic insulation material or goose down;* and thirdly, a waterproof cover or ground sheet to protect the sleeping bag on the top and bottom and adequately large to be pulled up around the face and perhaps cover your pack as well. I have a fitted cover for my bag with a pocket in its bottom for the ground pad. An oversized poncho built to cover a pack as well, also works quite well. So long as you have

these three pieces of equipment it is generally possible to sleep outside under quite severe winter conditions and remain comfortable. The addition of a tent can replace the waterproof outer protection and makes the whole experience far more comfortable when any wind or precipitation is expected. The first item of equipment, the ground pad or ground insulator, is best found in the form of approximately $\frac{1}{2}$ inch thick closed cell foam pads. "Ensolite" is one of the more popular forms of foams. The urethanes and neoprenes are also used. The important factor is that the construction is *closed celled* so as not to absorb water. The amount of softness in the pad is really not a critical factor as one quickly becomes accustomed to sleeping on quite a firm bed. When tired, simply dropping the bag in some soft snow will provide a fairly resilient and comfortable surface on which to sleep. In wilderness areas it is often a good idea to make a bed of small boughs from coniferous trees which will provide some insulation from the cold of the snow and also some softness. However, again, this should not be practiced anywhere but in extremely remote wilderness areas that others will not likely visit for years. Actually, one becomes very accustomed to the ground on which one sleeps and it isn't really necessary to have more than the foam insulator pad beneath you. These three items of equipment then, pad, bag, and cover, are critical to maintaining your comfort while travelling in the winter.

*The pros and cons of goose down vs. the synthetics are numerous. Down is warmest and lightest if kept dry. The synthetics are warm even when wet. Most serious expedition skiers are now using synthetics with a light, summer weight down liner.

Figure 8.19 In the cave. Note the ski pole in vent hole.

Figure 8.17 Digging a Snow Cave

Figure 8.18 Digging is always warm work and it is difficult to avoid getting wet.

Figure 8.20 Keeping warm simply requires using your head.

In the morning, after you have used your pad and cover, simply hang them in the air where the moisture on their surfaces from any condensation can quickly freeze. Then give it a few flops in the air and this condensation will come off in a form of frost, leaving the pad and cover very dry and ready to re-roll for the next night. The bag itself must be properly constructed for winter use. The cross baffle technique is important where no stitched seams penetrate from the outside of the bag to the inside allowing heat to escape very easily. Inexpensive summer bags use this type of construction but they are quite inappropriate for winter camping. The loft of the bag is important and should be maintained by carefully fluffing it before use.

Down bags having 2 to 4 lbs of down in them usually can have a loft of upwards of 4 to 6 inches of height or thickness measured on the top of the bag when one is in it. While a mummy bag is the best shape for keeping warm in the winter, the outer bag cover should not be of the same configuration. A conventional rectangular cut is far superior as this will allow the cover to stay in position when you roll or turn during the night within your mummy bag. If you were to have a fitted cover which rolled with you, the snow could work its way into the wrinkles in the cover. It would then melt due to your escaping body heat and penetrate the cover causing the bag to become wet. It's far better to have the outer cover light and loose and not connected to the bag in any physical way. The cover, again, should be of a breathable but reasonably waterproof material. One assumes that if you are sleeping outdoors without the protection of a tent, the cover must prevent the penetration of snow, not rain. Sleeping outdoors in the rain without a tent and keeping your sleeping bag dry is virtually an impossibility because if you use a rubberized or totally waterproof outer cover the condensation which forms inside it will almost invariably soak the bag. I think that over the years we will perhaps see a contained sleeping bag cover which can somehow be spaced away from the bag and ventilated in such a way that this problem will be eliminated. But as yet, no such piece of equipment exists. I recommend that you have a sleeping bag cover, or double bag cover, sewn up from about 3 ounces per yard nylon or cotton polyester material. It will be adequate to keep light or drifting snow from contacting the down sleeping bag and getting it damp. Its primary function is really as a windbreak. While utilizing some already existing article of clothing for this protection is best, one seldom would need a rain poncho on a mid-winter ski tour. Better to design and make your own bivouac sack to serve this function. It is always good to have this item along.

In the morning remove the outer cover and scatter the frost. This will allow it to dry almost immediately and be suitable for rerolling the sleeping bag in.

The satisfaction of being able to travel completely self-contained with your sleeping bag, its ground pad and cover, and all essential clothing within the bag is great. It reduces the number of objects to be carried in your ruck-sack.

When sleeping in the open, snow can actually be allowed to fall on your face, even drift completely over your face. A dome-like space will be formed by your exhalations. Often the snow will span a foot or more and allow you to turn your head as you roll in the night and still won't get in your face or get you wet. In fact, as the drifting over occurs, you heat up this dome-like space and remain very comfortable. It is very quiet and an ideal form of protection. You need not worry about a lack of oxygen because ample oxygen can penetrate the very light snow that is likely to form in the course of a night. Should it drift to some thickness, poke out a breathing hole periodically. Emerging from the snow in the morning warm, dry and comfortable, gives one an immense feeling of satisfaction at coping with the elements.

KEEPING WARM IN THE COLD

In the preceding pages I have outlined many ways to keep warm by eating warm food, dressing properly, and seeking shelter from weather and cold. Succeeding in staying warm under adverse conditions is inevitably something one continues to get better at with experience.

A few words about keeping warm in a sleeping bag are in order. The first rule is that one should sleep completely nude in any bag. Dressing and undressing entirely within the bag is normally possible for most people. The theory here is that the air layer around your body is warmed to virtually skin temperature in a good bag and you are completely free to turn and roll in your sleep minimizing the amount of skin that is in actual contact with the bag fabric. Heat losses through conduction are, therefore, less than they would be if you kept your clothes on.

You are undoubtedly wondering how on earth one can sleep nude in a sleeping bag in mid-winter what with the problems of going to the bathroom and dressing. Actually undressing in the bag *is* exercise and gets you nicely warmed up (and the air layer around you) before you attempt sleep. I've never found dressing in the morning to be a problem because as you warm up you can come out of the bag. It is important in very severe weather to avoid getting up to relieve oneself in the middle of the night because aside from being a very unpleasant experience, one tends to return to the bag chilled. If it becomes essential, dress entirely as if you were getting up to begin a new day.

Bringing a plastic bag into the sleeping bag with you makes it possible to relieve oneself without going outside. This is even possible *and* practical for women although most who have never tried it will insist that I am wrong on this.

Should you wake in the night shivering, try eating a small piece of chocolate which will fuel your body fire and make you feel warm almost immediately.

Clothing should be stored in the bag, or under it, as a pillow, where it will be warm and dry to put on in the morning. Completely soaking wet socks can be dried entirely in one night loose in a sleeping bag. If you have some precious object which has become wet (such as wooden matches) try sticking it in your hair. Within a few hours it will be dry as a bone!

Ski boots must be kept in or under the sleeping bag as well to be comfortable in the morning. Cold boots can mean cold feet for an entire day.

COLD INJURIES

It is wise for anyone skiing anywhere to be thoroughly familiar with the dangers of cold injury so that he or she may deal with them if necessary. Try as we do to avoid emergencies it seems that, inevitably, one is likely to encounter them. Cold emergencies often take place in the summertime as well as the winter. Getting lost and extending your exposure far past your expectations is the commonest cause followed by unexpected changes in the weather. I list below some of the possible consequences of getting cold:

1) *Frostnip* is surface freezing which precedes deep frostbite. It can normally be recognized as a blanching of the skin or white spots. These commonly appear on the face on a cold day with extreme winds. Soft sensitive skin freezes more quickly than toughened skin. General physical well-being and diet has a lot to do with it as well. If you are run down and tired you are more susceptible. Hands, face, and feet should not be washed excessively before going into the cold. This removes a protective layer of skin. Shaving should be done with extreme care to avoid removing skin, in otherwords do *not* try for a close shave. On a prolonged trip shaving should be put off for 2 or 3 days. Full beards often accumulate ice which can lead to further injury. Simply an unkempt, recently unshaven appearance is your best defence! On a ski tour you should check each other constantly for blanching in the face, especially young children who tend not to notice it on themselves. If detected, simply place a warm hand over the spot until it thaws and try to improve the face protection on the skier.

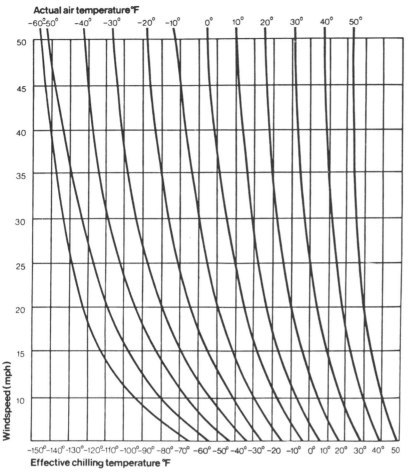

Figure 8.21 Wind Chill Chart; Follow the known temperature line to the point where it intersects with the wind speed line and read directly down for effective chilling temperature. (Chart courtesy of Museum of Science, Boston, Mass. / Kamlish)

the skin or immediate sub-cutaneous tissues and, depending on ambient temperature or wind chill, the required time of exposure ranges from a few seconds to several hours. If previously frostbitten you are generally more susceptible to further cold injury depending upon the amount of permanent tissue damage.

I once suffered deep frostbite in my entire right hand (the one holding my ice axe) after a bivouac at 21,000 feet on Huascaran in the Cordillera Blanca of Peru. The hand remained frozen most of the day while descending to our high camp. There it was rewarmed using body heat and I tied it in a sling. Within 8 to 12 hours it swelled to 3 times normal size in a giant watery blister. I was extremely careful not to puncture this blister during the rest of the descent and for the 2 weeks or so it took to subside. I was then left with an apparently lifeless hand which turned dark brown and was as hard as a piece of wood. I kept it in a sling for some 2 months and gradually the brown dead tissue began to be replaced by new tissue from the base of the hand. After six months the new tissue reached the extremities of the fingers and I was completely back to normal! I am convinced that it was my fanatical care in avoiding infection which promoted faster healing (I also refused to allow Peruvian doctors to drain the blisters). For the first 2 or 3 winters afterwards my hand seemed to get cold quicker than usual but today I notice no difference at all.

The major things to remember about frostbite are: no rubbing, no excessive heat in rewarming, and protect the area from rupture and infection.

2) *Deep Frostbite* effecting not only exposed facial tissues but extremities such as ears, fingers, and toes, is the next step beyond frostnip. Damage can be severe and nearly instantaneous under extremely low temperatures. If wearing a sufficiently bulky parka, frostbite of the hands can be forestalled by rewarming each hand under the opposite armpit.

Feet can be warmed by placing them between the legs of a companion. Warming the heels will promote warming of the toes more rapidly. Never rub or massage frostbitten areas. Gently rewarm with body heat or ideally a water bath of 104°F to 109°F (40°C to 42°C) although this is seldom available in the field! Frostbite results from crystallization of tissue fluids in

3) *Immersion foot* results from long periods with wet feet in temperatures from 68°F (20°C) down to freezing. It is quite rare and should always be possible to avoid. Immersion foot victims are very prone to subsequent cold injury.

4) *General Hypothermia:* at environmental temperatures less than 68° to 70°F (20°C to 21°C) survival depends upon insulation (body fat and clothing), ratio of body surface to volume, the body "fire" basic metabolic rate, and the will to survive. When the body core temperature falls below 95°F (35°C) hypothermia produces diminished BMR, heart rate, blood pressure, and uncontrollable shivering. Hallucinations, apathy, and narcosis occur at core temperatures of 86°F to 75°F (30°C to 24°C). Those that have nearly died of hypothermia describe the symptoms as follows: extreme fatigue causing sleep even while shivering; weakness; joint stiffness; and finally a feeling of warmth, comfort, and sleepiness. To another person the symptoms appear as irritability, irrationality, clumsiness, heavy speech, bluish lips, breathing difficulties, over dilated pupils.

Mild cases will recover if the victim is wrapped in blankets or a sleeping bag and is allowed to rewarm from his own metabolic heat production. Severe cases will die unless this rewarming is more active such as immersion in a tub of water at 105° to 110°F (40°C to 41°C) or a hot shower until all shivering has stopped.

Preferably such active rewarming should be performed under the supervision of a doctor. Rewarming of the exterior of the body can actually induce a further and often fatal drop in the internal temperatures. For this reason warm fluids should be given any conscious victim to internally warm him at the same time. Rescue units are now utilizing preheated oxygen breathing mixtures to treat hypothermia victims and are experiencing a high proportion of success.

Fortunately most healthy people fully recover from even severe hypothermia if treated properly. Often when one reads about those who have succumbed to hypothermia it comes to light that they were overtired and in poor health before even being exposed to the cold. Those dying from hypothermia are often diagnosed as having pulmonary edema (altitude-caused fluid in the lungs) due to lung congestion that accompanies the final symptoms of this injury.

5) *Cold Volatile Fluids:* serious permanent eye injuries can occur from being splashed with high volatile fluids (such as cooking stove fuel) under extremely cold temperatures. Until medical treatment arrives, flush with water warmed to 70° to 80°F (21°C to 23°C). Avoid all rubbing. A few drops of mineral oil or olive oil may be used for additional relief. Gasoline can cause instant frostbite if splashed on bare skin. It should be handled with utmost care.

6) *Snow Blindness:* extreme sunshine on white snow can cause snow blindness. It is most prevalent in cloudy or "white-out" conditions when there are no shadows, no relief for the eyes. The victim feels as if his eyes are filled with sand and the pain intensified with eyeball movement, watering, redness, headache, and even more pain when exposed to light. Treatment should include blindfolding and complete rest. Healing normally occurs within a few days but the eyes will remain susceptible to bright light for up to 5 years or more.

7) *Frostbite of lungs:* during hyperventilation following strenuous exercise in extremely cold air below -25°F (-31°C) blood is often coughed up from the tracheabronchial tube. The condition is aggravated at high altitudes. An asthmatic condition may follow for several days. Prevention, by means of breathing through a face mask, balaclava, or deeply recessed parka hood, is the only treatment.

Wind Chill

Temperature is not the only determinate of coldness. The combination of wind and temperature produces the greatest heat loss and discomfort. With a wind speed of 20 mph a temperature of 5°F (-15°C) is just as effective in chilling the body as a temperature of -40°F (-40°C) with a very slight wind of less than 2 mph. Figure 8.21 illustrates the relationship of wind and temperature to produce effective chill factors.

When skiing, cold injuries are most likely to befall those who are not keeping muscularly active and are tired. Being physically fit is a prime requirement for keeping comfortable in the cold.

Diet plays little part in cold prevention. A normal individual living in a cold environment consumes proteins, carbohydrates, and fats in about the same proportion as in temperate conditions. Carbohydrates are quick energy foods. An ounce of beef fat contains 80% more calories than the same weight of sugar or lean beef. A greatly increased consumption of lean meat or carbohydrates cannot be tolerated by the normal individual unless accomplished by a corresponding increase in fat. Living in the cold requires considerably more food for each person due to the increased physical demands being placed on the body.

Under conditions of extreme cold and with continuous outdoor exertion man has a daily calorie requirement as high as 5,000 or more. Most people have a strong desire for fats as well.

SAFETY PRECAUTIONS

In summary, I offer the following basic rules for preventing cold injuries:

1. Carry emergency clothing under all circumstances sufficient to keep you *dry* as well as warm.

2. Carry emergency shelter or tools for constructing shelters when conditions may demand it.

3. Carry warming and nourishing foods of high calorie content. Avoid dehydration which speeds the onslaught of exhaustion, hypothermia, frostbite, altitude sickness, etc. Do not drink alcoholic beverages or smoke, both of which retard circulation.

5. *Anticipate* becoming cold. Put on extra clothes *before* you absolutely need them, not after.

6. Seek shelter early before you have become too exhausted to properly protect yourself.

7. Constantly check on one another for frostnip and frostbite or the onset of hypothermia.

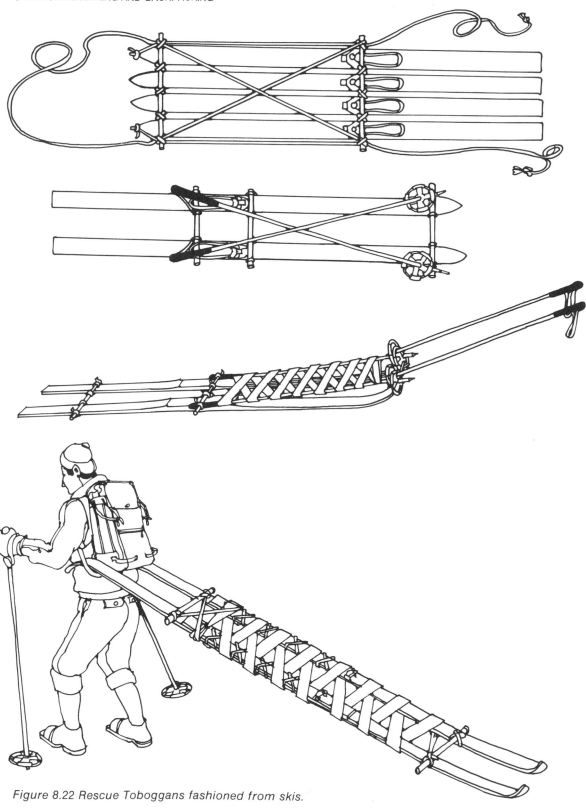

Figure 8.22 Rescue Toboggans fashioned from skis.

RESCUE

In the event of any injury great care must be exercised to insure that no further injury takes place. In large parties it is usually wise to bring the victim out with the party; while in small ones it generally is better to send two or more for help leaving the victim and at least one behind. It is apparent, therefore, that parties smaller than four have a significantly higher risk exposure in the event of an injury.

Reliance on public rescue organizations is very risky in spite of the superb achievements that many of these organizations have accomplished in the past. The very high cost of publicly funded search and rescue operations makes it, in my judgement, morally mandatory that any party entering wilderness areas in the winter be completely self-sufficient even to the extent of rescuing an injured person.

Notwithstanding the above, it is also essential that these agencies be notified of any intended expedition so that they can be effective if required. One should always bear in mind the fact that each time one calls on the aid of public rescue organizations, one is giving further credence to the concept that these organizations should have the right to decide whether or not a party should be permitted to enter a wilderness area in the first place.

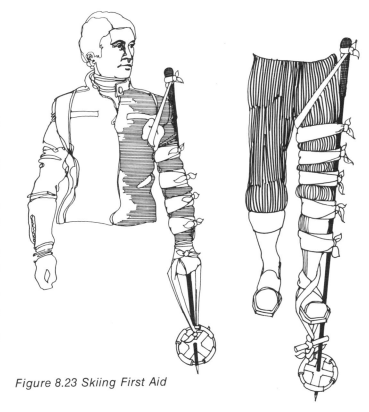

Figure 8.23 Skiing First Aid

CHAPTER NINE

SKI MOUNTAINEERING OR SKIING IN HAZARDOUS TERRAIN

ROUTE FINDING

Unfortunately no book can really teach the intricacies of selecting the proper route in hazardous terrain. The best way to learn is to ski with more experienced persons and constantly ask them why they choose to go one way rather than another. In mountaineering I've often placed tracing paper over a photo of a mountain and drawn dotted lines over possible routes indicating the intervals for required camps and estimated climbing times and then compared my results with others doing the same thing. Much is learned in this way.

Route finding is for me, one of the great joys of ski touring. Even planning a pleasant day's ski tour with children or inexperienced skiers is a challenge. Remember that all terrain can be dangerous if you get lost. I've gotten "lost" in a suburban housing development on skis in a snowstorm. I got so turned around that I was damned if I could find where I'd left my car! There was never any real danger of course as we could have knocked on any door, but even then I don't think I would have known the name of the road that I had parked on! As it was, we eventually found the car but at least 1½ hours after we should have stopped skiing. This kind of experience can make you feel very dumb indeed. It can also tell you something about the real danger of becoming lost in the wilderness. Being overdue at your campsite, missing a rendez-vous with another party – all of these complications can result from becoming lost or seriously underestimating your rate of progress.

In this section I will outline some of the general principles and techniques of route finding and

following as they apply to all forms of cross-country skiing.

1. On day tours always know the name of the road where you parked your car and the nearest intersecting road! A name on a nearby mailbox may be good enough.
2. Do not take young children or inexperienced skiers on an exploratory route which you have not skied before unless you are very very certain of the nature of the terrain *and* unless you deliberately grossly over-estimate your travel time, *and* unless you have absolutely predictable weather (ever seen that in North Eastern Canada/US?)
3. In exploring new routes use a map and compass.
Topographical maps available from the U.S. Geological Survey, Mapping Office Bethesda, Maryland and the Department of Mines, Mapping Division, in Ottawa, Ontario are usually quite adequate if large scale editions (1:25,000 is ideal) are used. It is no good to simply have a map and compass along. You must

pull them out regularly and mark your location on a continuous basis.

I once set out to ski around Mt. Tremblant in the Laurentians with a party of about 10 quite strong skiers. It was to have been a 20 mile trip or so. We started out behind our leader who was superconfident of the route. After many hours had passed and the landscape did not seem to develop the way it should have, discussions began about whether or not we should turn back on our own trail. Believe me this is one of the toughest decisions to have to make and the few times I have done it, it has proved to greatly prolong the length of the trip. In this case the dissension in the group allmost reached mutinous proportions as the weather began to deteriorate into blizzard conditions and our trail was gradually covered. I quite enjoyed it as I was almost keen to spend the night out anyway. However, our leader persevered and a few hours later we were surprised to come across our own trail. We had circumnavigated an entirely different mountain! All this would have been avoided if we had

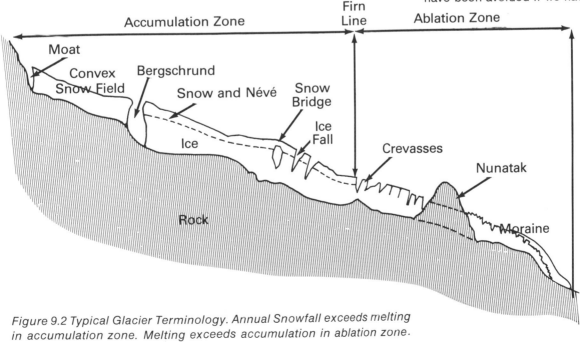

Figure 9.2 Typical Glacier Terminology. Annual Snowfall exceeds melting in accumulation zone. Melting exceeds accumulation in ablation zone.

constantly verified our position by bearings on other hills visible at first, or by the direction of slopes and stream beds. It is a great temptation to go "just a bit further" to see if the route turns out as expected.

4. Plan the route to include varied terrain but with a large part of the climbing positioned in the middle of the time span. These are the most satisfactory since you are warmed up during the meal break and have a downhill run to conclude the trip. I nearly always plan a trip to include a climb to high ground from where an exciting descent can be made. Following one's own tracks back is the safest way of doing this and one I highly recommend to anyone planning their own ski tours for the first time. It is quite easy to estimate the return time. If the terrain is flat but the conditions are slow breaking trail, your time back can still be cut nearly in half. Time savings on the return trip if it is a descent are all the more dramatic. A word of caution: sometimes weather can cause your trail to disappear; wind can fill in a track in soft snow within a few minutes, so take due precaution. Either place wands to mark your trail in exposed areas or choose a route which will keep your track protected from the wind.

I once arrived at a race site a day early in order to run the 30 km (18½ mi) course in a leisurely way simply to limber up and learn the trail. I set off at 1 PM on a sunny day expecting to certainly be back by dark. But as is so often the way, the track was poorly marked and after about 2

Figure 9.3 Glacier Crevasse Characteristics. Open and hazardous glacial crevasses are always perpendicular to ice flow direction. Tight pressure cracks tend to align with ice flow direction.

hours I concluded that I had lost it. Returning reluctantly on my own trail I came to a lake where my track had disappeared. I skirted the far shore and could find not a trace of where I had started across the lake! It took several more hours, well after dark, before I finally came out on a road and flagged down a car some 14 miles (22.5 km) from my starting point! I was so cold and so exhausted that racing the next day was out of the question. But I had learned, the hard way, how easy it is to lose one's trail!

5. Plan your route to avoid very steep up-grades. Try to make long traverses following a natural and consistent grade. I often make an ascent this way and then descend directly on the fall line telemarking across my trail up at intervals. Plan your route to stay out of the wind (see Chapter One). Consider your lunch spot in advance; will there be a dry spot to sit down; will there be sun; will there be shelter if it is snowing or raining?

6. Route finding above timberline exposes one to avalanche and crevasse hazards as well as more severe consequences from changes in the weather. It is therefore a much more formidable problem. The best possible way to plan a tour above timberline is to have recent, low altitude oblique aerial photos to work from. Topographic maps are the second best thing, but in poor visibility they are difficult to rely on. If you have good aerial photos study them with a magnifying glass (or stereo glasses if they are of the high altitude dimensional type) and note all landmarks such as rock outcroppings, bergshrunds, ridge lines, cornices, glacial centerlines, avalanche slope centerlines, and the like. It is wise to sketch your own map annotating all of these and dotting in your proposed and alternative routes. Note sections where you expect to ski roped up. Note also all points of shelter, possible water sources, and alternative descent routes. When you start, constantly refer to your map and plot your position. I carry maps and compass in the chest pocket of my anorak at all times so that it is not even necessary to stop in order to refer to it. These, then, are general aspects of route finding above timberline.

7. Aside from the above general consideration and the necessity for staying out of crevasses and avalanches, route finding above timberline is very similar to below. Ski touring enables one to take quite different paths than one would consider in summertime. For instance, in the summer a ridge route offers all kinds of advantages being easy to follow in a white-out, etc; while traversing a scree slope in the summer is very slow and awkward. In the winter exactly the opposite is true. Traversing, both ascending and descending, is the easiest way to go. Ridges are usually blown clear of snow or contain dangerous cornices. However, traversing a large snow field in white-out conditions can easily cause you to become lost. You are *lost* when you do not know *exactly* where you are! It is wise to ascend on one side of a valley having to cross the center water course or glacier as seldom as possible. In choosing the side to ascend on, bear in mind avalanche conditions. The windward side of a ridge is far likely to be safer, the snow being less deep and therefore more stable, the ridge crest free of cornices. If you opt to follow a ridge, stay well down on the windward side completely clear of the fracture line of cornices, if there are any. Sometimes in poor visibility it is extremely difficult to discern the cornices. The snow blows off into the white sky making the junction between ground and air undistinguishable. One day in March, while making an early ski ascent on Mount Washington, I remember linking ski poles together to form a chain and grasping this, crawling on my hands and knees hand and knees towards the edge of the cornice line to see if a descent in that direction would be possible! When my feet broke through the edge I could look down 20 feet or more to the steep slope below! Needless to say we found another way to descend.

8. Valley ascents to a col and then a descent into another valley for the return are some of the most enjoyable above timberline tours, but also involve extremely good (and current) knowledge of the descent side. They should therefore never be attempted by a novice route finder. Far better to have seen the country you will ski down on the way up. Don't forget that the winter landscape changes continually above timberline, and dramatically so where glaciers or ice falls are involved. When climbing, always turn around to get a mental picture of what the route looks like when coming down. Note landmarks and place warning wands where danger lies. Don't forget that a snow flurry or cloud could cut visibility on the way down.

If it is necessary to ski on a glacier, and any snowfield should be considered to be a glacier unless you know absolutely the depth of the snow and the hazard of a crevasse, substantial precautions must be taken. Generally I would consider glacier travel in the realm of mountaineering. Late season descents using alpine equipment can often be made in relative safety without extra equipment; but any route across glaciated terrain covered with fresh snow requires the utmost caution. Techniques for this are covered in the section on *Crevasse Hazards*. From a route-finding standpoint there are a number of things to bear in mind.

First of all, have a good mental image of the direction of ice flow so that you can visualize predominant orientation of crevasses. Study any glacier which you intend to cross from a distance with binoculars and pick your route. Make a sketch of prominent landmarks along the way. Once out on the ice the landscape can turn into a bewildering maze of séracs, dead end routes terminated by intersecting crevasses, and the like. Remember when ascending that the descent must be practical on skis while roped. Before attempting to pick a route on a glacier, yourself, do it with an experienced guide and have him criticize your decisions. Select a route with minimum exposure to objective hazards such as ice fall or avalanches.

Remember: any glacier is a moving, changing, and unpredictable phenomenon. Do not count on snow bridges used on the ascent to be there when you return. For this reason never, if possible, camp directly on a glacier where a crevasse can appear in moments.

Routes on glaciers are often necessary; often beautiful. They are often faster than the routes on the glacier borders which are usually rough and sometimes exposed to avalanche risk or debris. Go slowly when assuming the responsibility for leading a party on a glacier. Research the glacier's formation and movement patterns so you can anticipate, at least to some degree, its varying structure. Never venture on a glacier unless you and all members of your party have been trained in crevasse rescue. Trained means having *practical experience* not simply having read about the method!

Figure 9.4 *White-out conditions can arrive in seconds in the mountains.*

WEATHER HAZARDS

The cross-country skier is exposed to weather changes from as minimal as the loss of the warming sun due to a sudden cloud cover on a springtime tour, to violent blizzard white-out conditions arriving within moments in the mountains.

Weather knowledge of the areas in which you are skiing is essential. Knowing the conditions which are possible and being prepared for them, is the primary responsibility of the party leader.

In the coastal ranges of the world, snow storms can last for literally weeks, making ski expeditions in those areas extremely costly due to the provisionary requirements.

I would say that the best ski touring conditions are always in areas where the weather can change dramatically. In New England, people always say, "If you don't like the weather, just wait five minutes"!

The skier must be prepared for all eventualities.

AVALANCHE HAZARDS

The true nemesis of the deep snow skier must be the avalanche. Without this hazard, skiing above timberline would be infinitely safer. Like glaciers, avalanches cannot be analyzed and expected to behave exactly per that analysis. This explains the large number of deaths we read about of experienced mountaineers dying in avalanches annually. In these pages it is hoped that the reader will at least gain some appreciation of the probability of avalanches under different conditions; what to do if caught; and how to search for a lost companion.

Properties of Snow

Before attempting to learn the signs which accompany avalanche hazard, it is well to appreciate some of the mechanical and thermal properties of snow. Snow crystals of a variety of types (see Figure 9.5) result whenever precipitation occurs at temperatures below freezing. The density of newly fallen snow usually depends on the crystal type and the air temperature. The lightest snow falls when it is cold with no wind; the heaviest when it is close to freezing. The mechanical strength characteristics of different types of snow vary widely. The density of snow alone ranges over a scale of 50,000 to 1.

In Chapter Six we learned about the metamorphosis of snow. Those beautiful stellar crystals which you see floating down on a cold still night gradually break down into small round balls of ice after a period of time. The process is extremely rapid near the freezing point and hardly happens at all below -40°F (-40°C.) This is known as "destructive metamorphosis" and it happens only on snow which is of a reasonably uniform temperature. This is the most common condition.

Another type of metamorphosis is called temperature-gradient or "constructive metamorphosis" which occurs as water vapour migrates through the snow mass. In this case ice crystals are formed which entirely transform the original snow crystals previously undergoing destructive metamorphosis. A very fragile "structure" is often formed within the snow by this process (depth hoar or "sugar" snow) which becomes soft and mushy when wet. For constructive metamorphosis to occur, a steep temperature gradient within the snow is required, due to an extreme weather change causing water vapour to diffuse inside the snow layer. Usually this occurs early in the season before the snow mass has been consolidated.

Snow on a slope creeps downhill like a viscous fluid causing stresses and strains within it due to uneven rates of flow and uneven slippage over the ground beneath it. Since its mechanical properties are constantly changing due to metamorphosis, it is constantly being shifted. This movement,

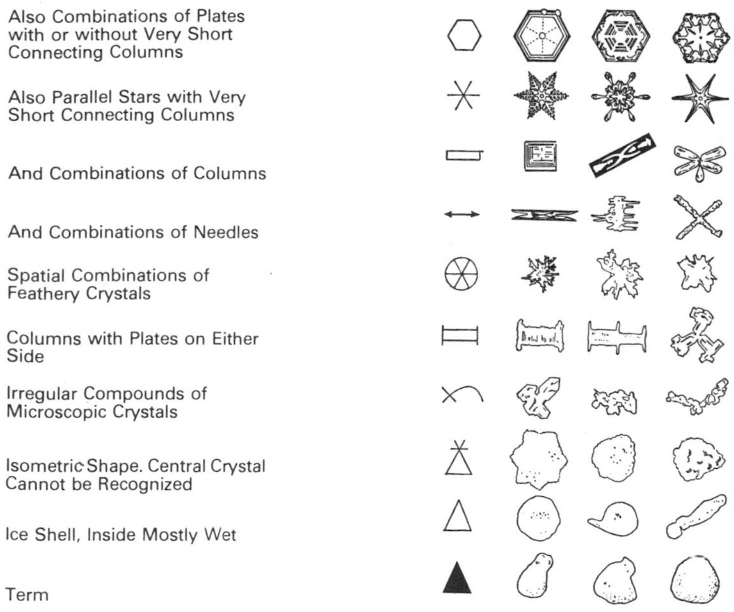

Also Combinations of Plates with or without Very Short Connecting Columns

Also Parallel Stars with Very Short Connecting Columns

And Combinations of Columns

And Combinations of Needles

Spatial Combinations of Feathery Crystals

Columns with Plates on Either Side

Irregular Compounds of Microscopic Crystals

Isometric Shape. Central Crystal Cannot be Recognized

Ice Shell, Inside Mostly Wet

Term

From International Snow Classification.

Figure 9.5 International Snow Classification. Types of metamorphosed snow.

followed by a period of "set", causes "age hardening". (Remember Chapter Eight preparing soft snow for igloo building? See p. 130)

Movement of snow crystals by wind is the principal cause of age hardening. Wind drifted snow is always firmer for this reason.

Snow and Heat
As we learned from building an igloo, snow is a fantastic insulator. In high school physics we were taught about its high latent heat of fusion (80 cal. to change 1 gram from solid to liquid with no temperature change). Water is remarkable also in its presence as a vapour, liquid and solid all at the same time. These three characteristics govern the manner in which a snow mass gains and loses heat.

At the base of the snow mass the ground temperature is almost always 32°F (0°C) due to the fact that higher temperatures exist within the ground and would melt the snow if the freezing point were not maintained at the surface. Heat

is transmitted to and removed from the snow mass primarily by these factors: turbulent air at its surface, long and short wave radiation, condensation-evaporation-sublimation, rainfall, and conduction.

Rain has perhaps the most rapid effect on the temperature of a snow mass since it causes a dramatic increase in conductivity. Very cold snow can be warmed to the freezing point in a matter of hours from a warm rain. Warm winds (such as chinook) can transfer the greatest amount of heat or melt the most snow. Radiation losses and gains are effected by cloud cover. When skies are clear, snow loses heat to space. When warm clouds or fog cover the sky, snow gains heat. Usually in winter, snow gains more heat than it loses during the day and loses more at night.

Through this brief introduction to the physical properties of snow one can see what a constantly changing medium it is. Hopefully by understanding its behavior or reaction to outside influences you will be better prepared for predicting its response.

147

TYPES OF AVALANCHES

Avalanches are either of *loose snow,* regardless of whether wet or dry, or of *slabs*. In the first type the snow starts to move at a single point and gradually starts more snow moving. The second type or slab avalanche is characterized by a mass of snow starting to move all at once and being relatively cohesive. Once moving, the slab avalanche may look quite like a loose snow avalanche. But if you look at its point of origin you will see the telltale fracture line, perpendicular to the fall line, running across its original breadth. Usually you can distinctly see the depth of the layer that slid. In a large slab avalanche large chunks and sometimes a whole tennis court size piece will remain relatively intact during its descent.

Loose Snow Avalanches
These arise when snow accumulates on a slope too steep for its natural angle of repose. It could be triggered by: (1) simple snow accumulation to too heavy a depth when there is no wind; (2) weakening of the snow due to metamorphic changes; (3) lubrication of the snow caused by percolating melt water. The more wet and dense the snow is, the greater the danger due to the tremendous inertia that a large quantity of snow may have even if travelling slowly. This is often enough to carry the avalanche far out on to the valley floor wreaking havoc on its way.

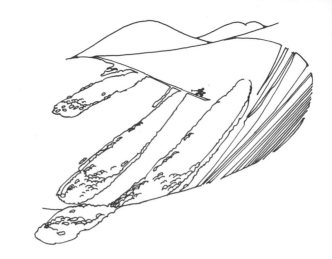

Large and small instability in loose snow.

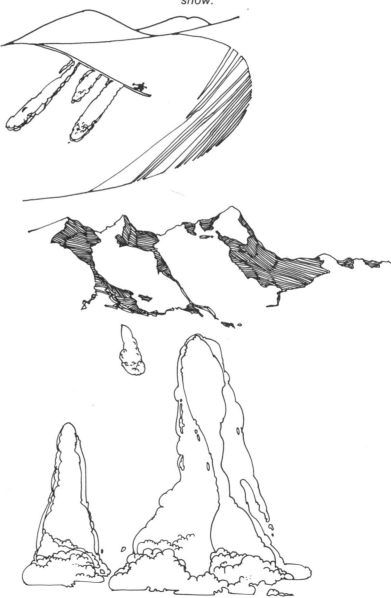

Figure 9.6 Loose Snow Avalanches.

Slab Avalanches

Slab avalanches are the most dangerous type of avalanche. Usually initiated by their own victims, they are characterized by a large mass or layer of snow beginning to move all at once. From what we have learned about the physical properties of snow it is apparent that the physical state of any snow layer can change rapidly and that the interface between one layer and another can also be transformed in such a way as to suddenly have its bond strength removed.

Often succeeding snow falls have an ice or wind-formed crust topping. This forms a perfect smooth sliding surface especially if lubricated by a thin snow film or deposit of surface hoar. Once a layer of snow lying on a steep slope becomes unstable it needs only slight force to set it moving.

Sometimes this force need only be a loud sound, invariably a single skier is adequate to destroy its equilibrium and set the mass in motion. The most frequent external natural triggering events are a small slide of loose snow totally harmless in itself, but possessing sufficient inertia to start a much larger unstable snow mass moving; falling snow cornices and ice and rock fall.

Internal natural triggering of a slab avalanche can occur simply by the changes in its snow layers as a result of: constructive metamorphasis; simple addition of new snow and consequently, weight; and temperature changes. These are far more subtle and therefore difficult to detect. Slab avalanches are generally categorized as hard or soft. Hard slabs are more localized areas densely compacted by very high winds. Soft slabs can result from

any of the causes indicated and over a much more general area.

In major alpine ski areas avalanches are often deliberately triggered by use of explosives. This can be quite effective in eliminating dangerous cornices and slabs which have become overloaded by snowfall during the night. It is by no means as effective in eliminating slabs which are internally in the process of becoming more unstable and which may be triggered later in the day. Slabs undergoing internal changes on convex slopes are subject to far more stress than those on concave slopes where consolidation tends to pull the slab together rather than stretch it out. The skier's track can be like a knife slicing off a slab. The skier in this respect is more likely to trigger a slab than would a climber.

Avoiding Avalanches

The safest areas are the ridges, but these are often bare of snow or exposed to high winds. The valley floor is next safest although often there is evidence of long reaching slide activity from one side or the other (usually not both). So stay as far away from that side as possible. Rough surfaced slopes with many rock out-croppings are next as being usually secure. Trees and other projections through the snow are usually an effective deterrent to any slide activity.

Slopes facing into the wind and sun are usually more stable than slopes in the lee or shadow. Snow deposited in high winds is tightly consolidated and much more stable than that deposited in calm or turbulent air common to ice slopes. All other things being equal, convex slopes are generally more dangerous than concave as far as slabs are concerned.

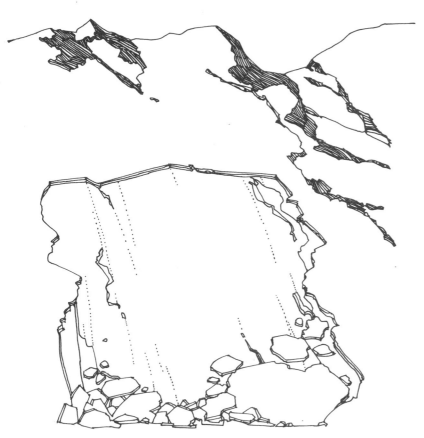

Figure 9.7 Slab Avalanche

It is not hard to recognize the physical ingredients for a potential avalanche and to avoid them. One must develop a good knowledge of the terrain and the manner in which snow is deposited on it. However, even in new terrain potential fracture zones become pretty obvious.

AVALANCHES AND WEATHER

Immediately after a heavy winter storm loose snow avalanche hazards are greatest and diminish rapidly with time as the snow settles and consolidates. The rate of this decline in hazard varies directly with temperature: most rapid (only 6 hours) near freezing; lasting for many days or weeks below 0°F (-18°C).

There are contributing factors which influence avalanche hazard following a storm. These are as follows:

Snow depth If the ground was bare prior to the storm the danger is least. If the snow was deep and the slopes very smooth, the danger is greatest.

Snow surface If the surface prior to the storm was a glazed crust, the danger is greatest; the hazard is lessened with increased roughness.

Amount of snow The greater the new snowfall, the greater the hazard. 4 inches or more is generally required to develop some threat, 8 inches to 12 inches to make it serious.

Types of snow Slabs do not normally develop from stellar or plate crystals (see Figure 9.5) unless driven by wind. Granular and needle crystals and graupel do form slabs easily.

Snow Density Fresh snow usually has a water content of 7% to 10%. Snow that is much more dense, say 30% water, readily forms dangerous slabs. Lighter snows, however, are extremely fragile and easily form loose snow avalanches.

Figure 9.8 Small (A) and large (B) instability in slabs

Snow fall rate Extremely rapid rates of deposition (eg. more than 1 inch per hour) increase slide hazard while slower rates (eg. less than $^1/_2$ inch per hour) are usually harmless.

Settlement After the new snow has fallen, if there is evidence of settlement or "sluffing" of the snow, it is an indication of stability. Lack of evidence is an indication of hazard. Small loose snow-slides on the surface usually indicate that settlement has occurred.

Wind New snow deposited in windy conditions nearly always forms slabs. Average velocities over 15 mph will guarantee it.

Temperature Rising temperatures during a storm will produce more instability than the reverse. Heavier more dense snow will be resting on lighter snow. I am always pleased with storms that begin as freezing rain and turn to snow thus insuring a good bond between the old and the new.

Hopefully this discussion of avalanche characteristics and factors contributing to their formation will give you at least some feeling for what causes them. Unstable loose snow whether dry or wet, and slabs whether soft or hard, can form in the subtlest of ways. A slope covered with earlier ski tracks can suddenly become hazardous due to the weakening of an earlier snow layer or the addition of melt or rain water increasing its density dramatically.

CROSSING AN AVALANCHE ZONE

Inevitably, crossing an area where you are suspicious of avalanche hazard will become a necessity. On skis there tend to be more such occasions than when climbing on foot. The reason for this is of course the skier's greater ability to traverse. Fortunately his ability to traverse at speeds is to his advantage. Other factors such as the continuity of his track are to his disadvantage. While a file of climbers all stepping in the individual steps kicked by their leader can often cross a slope without fracturing it, the single skier carving a continuous groove can fracture an entire slope which has tensile stress within it. Climbers ascending usually kick steps directly up a slope thus minimizing disruption of the stressed snow. The traversing skier is unable to do this.

Once placed in the undesirable position of having to cross a potential avalanche slope, there are a number of precautions to be taken:

1. *Cross One Man at a Time.* Never expose more than one to the hazard simultaneously.

2. *Cross quickly in a descending traverse.* To keep exposure to a minimum, ski as fast as you can with security, always being prepared for the dislodgement of a slab below you. Do not attempt to outrun an avalanche from above; it is far better to flatten your traverse in order to get out of its way as soon as possible.

Avalanche Facts

Avalanches are QUIET: No resounding roar foretells their approach. If you feel the shock wave of air, it is already too late.

Avalanches are POWERFUL: It has been calculated that some involve hundreds of thousands of tons of snow moving at speeds of up to 130 mph! *Skiers with skis on their feet:* They are more susceptible to being buried than they would be without their skis. Skis can also cause extreme twisting of the victim's legs.

A Victim's Chances of Survival: In wet snow avalanches, survival rates are less than 10% if totally buried. Even in dry snow unless the victims are found within an hour or less the chances of survival seldom rise above 20%.

Sound travel: Sound travels into the snow quite well, but a victim should never waste his energy trying to call to his rescuers since his efforts will inevitably be fruitless.

Figure 9.9

3. *Never try roped skiing.* In an avalanche area, there is no way to stop someone once caught in its force.

4. *Use avalanche cord.* At least 100 feet or red nylon parachute cord should drag behind each skier.

5. *Dress fully for immersion in the snow.* Put on hats, gloves and emergency clothing.

6. *Cross the slope as high as you can.* Carefully assess the consequences of a slide. If the slope funnels, thus concentrating the depth of any slide, or falls over a cliff, the risks may simply not be worth it.

7. *Look for islands of safety.* Look for such things as rock outcrops where you can rest as you progress across the slope.

8. *Unfasten pole wrist straps and loosen rucksack straps.* This will enable you to get rid of them if you are caught. These items, just as your skis themselves, can drag you under the snow surface if they become caught.

If caught in an avalanche the principal thing to attempt to do is to stay on top of it. This is best done by "swimming" on your back with your head up hill. Getting rid of your skis and rucksack are important first steps. As the slide slows down and it appears you will be buried move your arms in front of your face to create a breathing space. Avalanche snow feels like concrete immediately after it stops. Moving your body violently just in those final seconds can create space which will relieve snow pressure and provide breathing-air. Only in extremely dry snow avalanches is it possible to do much digging. Make certain you are digging *upwards* as some victims have been known to dig *down*. Sensing the effect of gravity on one's saliva is said to be a method of determining direction. In dry snow avalances breathing-air is more readily obtained but there is extreme hazard from inhaling snow into one's respiratory passages and lungs. Covering the nose and mouth is of extreme importance under these conditions. In wet snow, avalanche victims suffocate very quickly.

If you survive you must search for any victims *immediately* as every second wasted could spell disaster. Often victims lie just beneath the surface slightly lower than where they were last seen.

Send for help only if you have a large party and your initial search has been unsuccessful.

Mark the locations of any equipment found as these will be clues to the victim's location. Probe the snow with skis or upside down poles. Be careful not to use sharp objects. Ski mountaineering poles are available which screw into one another to form a long probe.

If buried, shouting is usually useless. Relax and do not use up excess oxygen by struggling.

First aid for a victim should be immediate. A R if he is not breathing and general treatment for shock.

Being buried in an avalanche, I can well imagine, is a frightening experience. I've been buried in a sand slide and the sense of helplessness is acute. Often when skiing I've triggered relatively harmless loose snow slides and have been able to ski out of them. Knowing when I should abandon myself to the slide and fight for survival, dumping my equipment, is not something I am 100% confident of. All too often in soft slab and loose snow slides one feels able to ski on the moving surface. Within seconds this can become impossible and those seconds could have been used in disposing of equipment.

Numerous electronic devices have become common for use when skiing in avalanche terrain. I highly recommend the use of such equipment in addition to an avalanche cord when skiing in a hazardous area. Basically these units are miniature transceivers broadcasting on a frequency of 22-75 hertz. They are worn in the "transmit" mode by all members of the party under their parka (*not* in their rucksack!). In the event of an avalanche the survivors all turn to the "receive" mode and by means of a highly directional receiving antenna they are able to locate victims through simple volume sensitivity.

It is very important that any party equipped with these devices *practice* using them before they are needed. All helicopter skiing in deep powder terrain is now done using these devices. One of the more popular units is the "Piep". Costs range from $45 to $65 depending on quantity. The size of the unit is 4 inches x 3 inches x 1 inch and its weight is 8 oz (266 g).

Avalanches are not to be trifled with. Read the accounts of accidents. Invariably improper assumptions were made about the stability of slopes. *Always* be suspicious and *always* be ready. There can be no other attitude towards the "white death".

Figure 9.10 Electronic Avalanche Victim Locator "Pieps 1" by Motronic (about $60)

Much of this information on avalanches comes from "The ABC of Avalanche Safety" and "A Field Guide to Snow Crystals" by Edward R. La Chapelle. Both of these volumes I highly recommend to anyone interested in improving their knowledge of the mechanics of snow.

CREVASSE HAZARDS

After weather and avalanche hazards, crevasses are the most serious threat to any tour skier venturing above timberline.

Bergshrunds: These are the large crevasses that ring the top of any large snow field or mass. As the snow consolidates it shrinks away from the upper convex slopes which are held by projecting rocks. The "shrund" usually opens just where the surface becomes concave. Skiing over a precipitous pitch where one cannot see the bottom always holds the danger of unexpectedly coming up on a bergshrund. They do have the nice feature however of the lower rim being substantially below the upper

Figure 9.11 Crevasse hazards are omnipresent wherever deep snow lies.

rim. It is therefore often possible to ski directly over one. If confronted with this sudden necessity it is best to turn towards the fall line and spring directly down it thus maximizing your jump and your margin for error. Invariably this will give you far too much speed and place you quite out of control or in an "egg beater" below the shrund, but this is better than going into it! Bergshrunds should be carefully inspected on the ascent. One should study their edges to determine the amount of overhang and the difficulty of crossing them safely on the descent.

The skiers has untold advantages over the climber when it comes to crevasse hazards. Because his weight is distributed over the length of his skis his chances of penetrating the snow and falling into a concealed crevasse are substantially lessened. Once in the crevasse, on the other hand, he could well be in more difficulty.

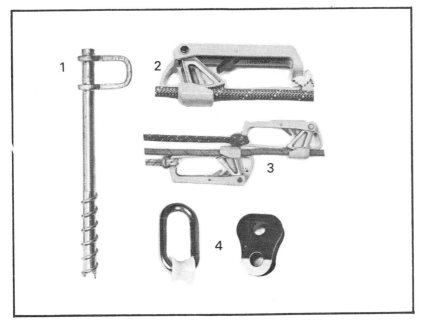

Figure 9.12 Some Equipment for Glacier Travel: (1) Salewa Tubular Ice Screw; (2) Jumar Ascenders to use in lieu of a Prussik Knot; (3) Pair of Jumar Ascenders; (4) Carabiner Rescue Pulley (see page 159 for a complete list of required items.)

153

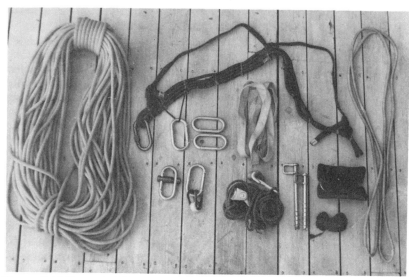

Figure 9.13 Essential Glacier Travel Equipment (Clockwise left to right) *60 meter x 11 mm climbing rope, chest harness with locking carabiner, seat sling, spare carabiners, Prussik sling, glacier glasses, avalanche cord, ice screws, ascenders, rescue pulley, and brake bar for rappeling.*

One of the great fascinations of snow and ice mountaineering for me has always been the fact that man could cross such seemingly impossible terrain as heavily crevassed glaciers completely covered in fresh concealing snow, in relative safety, simply by using proper techniques.

The tour skier enjoys this same ability but he must be prepared to contend with the extra equipment required. While his chances of actually falling in are lessened, he cannot ever ignore them. A fall into a crevasse is usually fatal if the climber or skier is unroped.

Thus the first safety rule: *Never ski unroped where a crevasse hazard may exist.* This rule is probably the most violated of all mountain skiing maxims. All people touring in the mountains, no matter how conservative, will expose themselves to objective hazards such as crevasses. The more knowledge they have, however, the less this exposure will be.

Since the technique of using a climbing rope, knots, slings, ice screws, belays etc., are beyond the scope of this book, I shall assume the reader has basic snow and ice mountaineering skills.

Roped skiing is usually carried on when ascending or travelling on relatively level terrain. To attempt downhill runs while roped is usually impractical although, in heavily crevassed terrain, it may still be necessary. It is well to consider the full consequences of roping up while on skis. While the climber with an ice axe and his two feet relatively firmly in the snow can reasonably be expected to arrest the downward plunge of a 200 lb. man 75 feet away as he falls into a crevasse, can the same be expected of a skier? I believe so, as the skis in a snow plow or sidestep position can offer very good purchase. I believe in a long rope for any glacier travel however, and would choose 60 meters of 9mm rope as opposed to perhaps 40 or 50 meters of 11 mm for a party of three. While travelling roped, one must be constantly aware of the implications of a fall by any party on the rope.

The second rule is: *Never approach crevasse hazards in such a way that more than one member of the party might fall in at once.*

Figure 9.14 Roped Skiing

Thus a 90° approach is best. If this is impractical, an echelon approach (see Figure 9.15) is the next best thing. At least this way more than one member on the rope will not end up in the same crevasse!

A third rule is: *Keep the rope fully extended at all times* unless an area of indisputable safety is evident. Do not carry large coils of rope in your hands which only mean your companion, should he fall, will free-fall that much further before you must arrest him. Often when skiing roped, a dynamic belay over a considerable distance may be needed. In this instance a large coil may be required but it should remain on the opposite side of the belayer from the skier!

Belay anchors either by means of a sling passed through an ice screw, or around two inverted ski poles driven in the snow, are definitely a good idea. Two ski poles pushed in the snow together in this way are 5 times as effective as a single pole. I discovered this as a carpenter driving nails . . . two driven together have considerably more holding and drawing power than one.

A fourth rule is: *Keep fully dressed, as in an area of avalanche hazard,* regardless of how warm it may be. Once suspended in a dark cold crevasse you will need all the warm clothing you have!

WATER AND ICE HAZARDS

Falling ice dropping from sun-warmed rock cliffs overhead and sliding down a snow field is a common late season hazard to tour skiers. The only protection is, first of all, to avoid such exposure where possible, but if this is not practical, to ski horizontally making as little noise as possible so as to be able to hear the tell-tale 'crack' as a piece of ice is dislodged. It is then a question of dodging it. I remember one day in Tuckerman's ravine on Mt. Washington when the exact location of the falling ice was concealed by a dense fog. One simply waited staring upwards into the whiteness ready to move left or right on first instinct as the block came into view. When they weigh several hundred pounds it is best to avoid being hit! We had no business being on those slopes under those conditions.

Watercourses beneath the snow can sometimes erode large tunnels in the spring run-off leading eventually to collapse of the snow structure spanning them. Great caution should be taken whenever you hear water in an open crevasse to be sure that it will not be *your* own weight which brings it all down.

Figure 9.15 Echelon Formation

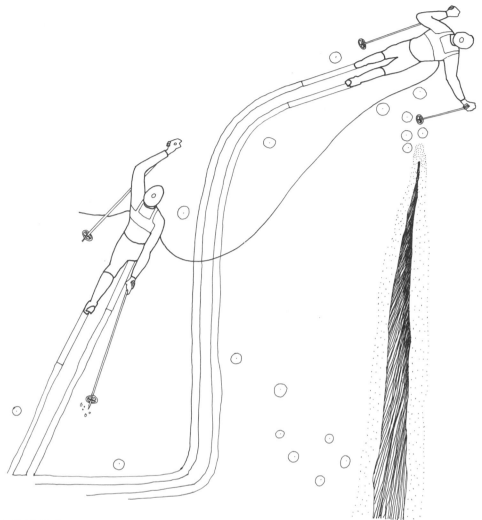

Figure 9.16 Going around a crevasse

Detecting Crevasses

The lead skier should keep a wary eye out for holes and any suggestion of sagging snow or linear depression that characterizes a snow covered crevasse. Sometimes extremely subtle discolourations in the snow makes these areas apparent. Flat light under white-out conditions or a noon sun can make spotting difficult. Low level morning or evening light is therefore far more preferable. The orientation of crevasses in any given area should be relatively easily identified. Once one crevasse is found, others usually parallel it not far away. The lead skier should probe ahead of his path firmly with his ski pole. Usually snow which will withstand these thrusts will not fail under the skier's skis. This is not something of which the climber probing with his ice axe can always be assured.

Surmounting a Crevasse

An end run is always the most desirable choice although sometimes it can seem to take ages to find the end. Always be conscious of the fact that the end is never the actual end, only the point where surface snow covers the gap in the ice. Crossing a narrow gap on skis is relatively easy. Approach at 90° and try to take enough run to insure your successful crossing even if one overhang should give way. Where a wider crevasse is bridged by snow at one place the problem is usually that one must descend to the snow bridge and then climb up the other side. Skiing rapidly onto the bridge in order to carry up the other side could place undue strain on the bridge. In this case it is better to traverse crossing the bridge on the bias, so that as little load as possible is placed on it. There is no substitute for a speedy crossing especially since on skis one is in a position to accomplish it. The belayer should get in a position where as little rope as possible need be extended in the dynamic belay. Often this means moving 90° from the general direction of the route. When the belayer is on the other side of the crevasse, as in the case of the last skier, this is particularly important since rope cannot be brought in as fast as the skier is likely to approach.

Extreme care must be taken by the belayer to insure that the skier is not pulled off balance by the rope. Due to the much higher relative speeds this can be much more difficult to prevent on skis than on foot.

The party on skis can move much more quickly than normal climbers. This very speed can spell disaster if everyone does not stay 100% alert since the number of crevasses encountered in a given period of time is that much higher.

Figure 9.17 Skiing over a snow bridge

Steep Slopes

While a mountaineer tries never to venture onto a slope upon which he cannot perform an effective self-arrest with his ice axe, the mountain tour-skier should never venture onto a slope which he cannot ski down competently and in control. Should the slope be beyond his ability to telemark or even to use alpine techniques, he may resort to a series of shallow traverses linked by kick turns.

Should he lose control of his position during any part of his descent he may require some self-arrest technique to prevent an extensive fall or a fall into hazardous terrain. Extending the arms overhead and attempting to scrape the snow with one pole grasped in both hands will usually bring the skier's feet beneath him. At this point the skis can be edged into the slope popping the sliding skier onto his feet. It is not easy; similarly an ice axe self-arrest is not easy. It is essential for anyone

venturing onto steep slopes that they practice deliberate falls on short slopes and develop an ability to regain their feet.

I do not believe the mountain skier should burden himself with an ice axe or attempt routes which are unskiable. Mixing mountaineering and skiing to this extent can spoil both. Very spectacular ascents can be made on skis without exposing oneself to extreme hazard or conditions requiring a belayed descent which so detracts from the pleasure of skiing.

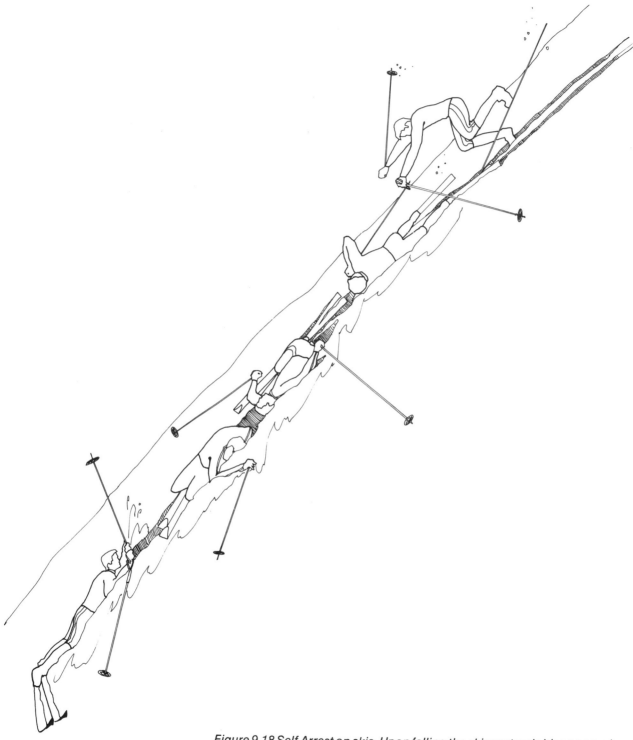

Figure 9.18 Self Arrest on skis. Upon falling the skier extends his arms and grasps one pole with both hands, driving either end into the slope so that his skis swing below him across the fall line. The skier can then remount his skis even while still moving.

EQUIPMENT REQUIREMENTS

Ski mountaineering equipment outside of skis, boots, poles, and winter camping gear is not elaborate. I would recommend the following items for a party of three skiers venturing into avalanche and crevasse terrain:

together:
1 – 60 meter (9 mm dia.) long climbing rope
50 – willow wands or more depending on the terrain
2 – rescue pulleys
2 – Jumar ascending clamps with slings for rescue operations

each man:
1 – chest harness seat sling and two carabiners (one locking type)
100 feet avalanche cord
1 – avalanche rescue transceiver set on "transmit"

Figure 9.19 Crevasse Rescue Operation: Two Prussik slings or ascenders can be used; one for hauling the skier on the rope, the other for holding the rope fast while the ascender or prussik is moved along the rope between pulls.

Figure 9.20 Methods for carrying skis: (1) bandolier style; (2) The easiest way – tied to one's rucksack; (3) Through the rucksack straps; (4) Over the shoulders on one's poles – the quickest way; (5) Suitcase style – as tiring as carrying a suitcase.

CHAPTER TEN
HISTORY

History

Cross-country skiing as we know it today is called nordic skiing (this also includes ski-jumping) because the past history of skiing has predominantly occurred in the nordic countries of Fenno-Scandia. It is interesting to look at the history of skiing because, in so doing, one can discover the reason why it has become as many faceted as it has.

Long before skiing became a sport, skis were a means of transport for the people living across Eurasia from Norway to China. There is considerable archeological evidence attesting to their antiquity. The oldest known ski is the so-called Hoting ski, which was found in a peat bog in Sweden and is presumed to be over 4,500 years old. In addition, rock paintings depicting skiers have been found (Figure 10.1) which date to 3000-2000 B.C. Also, Viking rune stones dating from circa 1000 A.D. depict skiers (Figure 10.2). The literary evidence of skiing is also considerable. The earliest reference occurs in the 6th century A.D. (see Chronology), when the skiing of the Finnish Lapps was described. There are many references to skiing which occur in the Norse sagas towards the end of the Middle Ages and we are fortunate to have illustrations of skiers in a book published in 1555; *"Historia de Gentibus Septentrionalibus"*, by Olaus Magnus of Norway.

THE EVOLUTION OF EQUIPMENT AND TECHNIQUE

The early evidence reveals a wide assortment of designs. At first, they were merely variations of the snowshoe, permitting the wearer to stand on top of the snow. They consisted of boards, or frames covered with skins or furs. Illustrations from Olaus Magnus depicted its wearers, the Lapps, hunting, making war and simply travelling. The skiers appear to use no poles and to be standing on the very tail of their boat-shaped skis. An illustration of a century later (Figure 10.3) shows Lapp skiers using skis of quite a different design. There is one long ski called the "Lang" or glide ski which was 9 to 11 feet in length, and a shorter, fur covered traction or pushing ski called the "Andor" which was 6 to 8 feet in length. A single long pole more than head high, was used for pushing. It was very stout and was covered with leather for several feet where it was gripped. This design was well adapted to enable the wearer to cover long distances across relatively flat northern terrain. One can only presume that these skiers switched skis at frequent intervals, or else developed heavily one-sided physiques. In the 18th century soliders using this equipment waged war in the northern European countries.

This form of skiing lasted well into the 19th century when Norwegians began to spread the practice of skiing around the world. In 1856 John A. "Snowshoe" Thompson began to carry mail across the Sierra Nevada Mountains in California on this type of ski and pole and continued to do so for 20 years.

Figure 10.2 Viking Rune Stone 1050 A.D.

The first downhill race occurred in Australia in 1861 at Kiandra. The participants were Norwegian miners who used the single pole as a brake while descending hills.

Gradually, ski equipment acquired specific characteristics which related to the terrain of each country. For example, the Norwegian push pole had a larger basket so as not to sink into the soft snow of their forests; the Finnish and Swedish versions had smaller discs for more crusted and windblown conditions. The Norwegian poles were shorter as well, with a wrist loop, while the Swedes and Finns had very long poles with oval shaped hand grips and curved spikes.

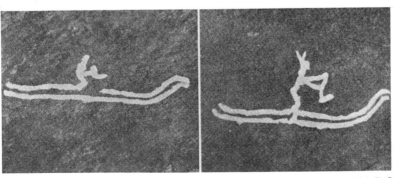

Figure 10.1 Norwegian Rock Painting Island of Rodoy 3000-5000 B.C.

The last 50 years of the 19th century witnessed very significant events in the history of skiing. These events and the individuals responsible for them changed the nature of skiing entirely and lead to its serious development as a sport. In this process, a schism developed between nordic skiing and its offshoot, downhill or alpine skiing, so that now, they are quite different in equipment and technique.

In the 1850's, Sondre Norheim from the village of Morgedal in Telemark, Norway, invented the first modern binding and in so doing, many believe, he revolutionized skiing. It is significant that this development occurred here, for it is an example of the adaptation of skis to suit the terrain. The topography of Telemark is decidedly rugged, particularly in comparison to most parts of southern Norway.

Down through the centuries, only toe bindings had been customarily used. They were straps either of leather, or of withe-willow twigs, or the roots of the birch tree. These primitive bindings had served the requirements of travel on flat, open terrain well enough, but skis with only a toe binding limited the development of technique. Even for the most adept, steering was hard and in Telemark, negotiating the rugged terrain required more control. Norheim's invention accomplished this. His binding fastened the foot more securely to the ski and at the same time, tremendously increased the freedom of movement. This binding was rigid strips of withe which not only formed the toe binding, but continued tightly and firmly around the heel of the boot. As a result of this invention, skiers found that they could now manoeuver their skis much more expertly and could execute intricate swings and turns.

Figure 10.3 Lapps making war on skis from **Olaus Magnus,** *1555*

Figure 10.4 Mediaeval representation of Korean skiers. Note the skis are worn in opposite fashion to those illustrated in **Olaus Magnus.**

More and more Norwegians began to ski for the sheer pleasure of it. In addition, at the same time the people of Telemark discovered that skis of equal length were most effective for handling their difficult terrain. They devised skis that were fairly short and slender which were about 8 cm wide at the front, tapered to about 7 cm in the middle and broadened to 7.5 cm at the back. By the 1890s the Telemark-type ski had caught on all over the country as had Norheim's binding. It should also be noted that Norheim was the first person to use 2 poles instead of one.

The first jumping championship occurred in Telemark in 1866, which Norheim won. In 1868, the annual ski jumping competition was inaugurated in Kristiania, as Oslo was then called, and Norheim won again, astounding the crowds by his demonstration of what he could do on skis. After this, he became a celebrity and demonstrated his skills as a jumper, slalom artist and cross-country racer in Telemark and at other skiing centers. His virtuosity did much to encourage new interest in ski technique. In 1879, the brothers Hemmestveit from Telemark

started the first ski school in Kristiania. Soon afterwards, the "Norwegian" sport spread to Switzerland and Austria.

Norheim did much to popularize skiing and later, in 1890, the famous Norwegian Arctic explorer, Fridtjof Nansen, was to greatly influence the spread of the sport outside of Norway. His book "First Crossing of Greenland" recorded his journey on skis across Greenland. It was very widely read, being translated into English, French and German. He attributes much of his success to the use of skis and records the technique and equipment used on his expedition, and some sensational distance and speed records attained by several of the Lapps who accompanied him. Among these were a reconnoitering expedition in which two of them covered 230 km in 57 hours. Nansen wrote; "Of all the sports in Norway, skiing is the most national in characteristic. As practised in our country, it ranks first in the sports of the world. Nothing hardens the muscles and makes the body so strong and elastic; nothing gives better presence of mind and nimbleness; nothing steels the will-power and freshens the mind as skiing. This is something that develops not only the body but also the soul – it has a far deeper meaning for people than many are aware of and a far greater national importance than is generally supposed."

Figure 10.5 18th century Siberian scene with dog sleds

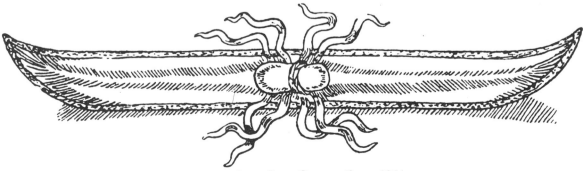

Figure 10.6 17th century Norwegian ski from **Saxo Grammaticus,** 1644.

In the closing decades of the 19th century, the sport spread to the Alpine regions of Switzerland and Austria, and new equipment and techniques were devised to adapt to the steeper terrain of alpine touring.

In the 1880s Matthias Zdarsky introduced Norwegian technique in the mountains near the village of Lillienfeld and there developed the fundamentals of alpine skiing with what was called the Lillienfeld technique. While Zdarsky still used the single pole, he did develop in 1892, a new binding in response to the steeper terrain of the Austrian mountains. He devised a sole binding, (Figure 10.17) in which greater heel control was attained by using a steel heel receptacle on the end of a spring steel sole plate. The heel was held in this socket by a strap over the instep, and the toe was restrained only by a strap linking two eyelets. The really important part of the unit lay ahead of the toe, however. It was a cylinder, housing a stiff, steel spring, whose tension could be varied. This held the sole plate down on the ski, but the heel could be lifted against the spring and this enabled the skier to kneel down on the skis with no strain on the foot. One advantage was that almost any kind of footwear could be used. Also, the newly acquired heel control was much better suited to turning on steep ground.

Figure 10.7 Lapps on the hunt from **Berdenmener,** *Hamburg, 1712*

Figure 10.8 18th century print depicting Samoyed natives. Note the horned toes on the mocassins which were fitted under the toe binding. It was not until the mid 19th century that an improvement on this arrangement was made.

In 1895, Fritz Huitfeldt, a Swiss, developed a binding which held the toe much more securely. He devised toe irons; the steel was about 10 inches long and 2 inches wide, and was inserted through a mortice in the center of the ski. A strap was passed through the slot in the iron and this served as a heel strap. Each end of the iron was then bent up and angled by wrenches to fit the sides of the boot sole. A toe strap was looped between the two upturned ends of the toe iron, and while the toe iron was very narrow, it was a vast improvement over a toe strap alone. Next was the problem of holding the boot reasonably firm within the jaws of the toe irons. The Ellesfen shortening clamp accomplished this (Figure 10.18). It was the forerunner of larger heel clamps such as the Bildstein, or the front-acting shortening clamps found on most cable bindings.

Figure 10.10 This illustration of 1820 attests to the fact that the Norwegian soldiers were proficient stick-riders.

Figure 10.9 18th century Norwegian soldier in uniform. The use of a single pole was retained in use for two reasons: 1) techniques for checking speed on the descent had not been developed; 2) a single pole made it easier to handle one's weapon, whether crossbow or rifle.

The Huitfeldt binding evolved further in the 1920s when Marius Eriksen provided a lip under which the edge of the sole was wedged, thus making toe straps unnecessary. Later, in the Alps in the 1930s, the Amstutz heel spring, devised by Walter Amstutz, held the heel down for christianias yet permitted it to be raised high in the telemark. The Bildstein heel clamp was another definite improvement, being a continuous spring on the cable around the heel with a shortening clamp integral with it. Finally, in the mid-thirties, the Kandahar cable binding and its variations superseded most of the other types for downhill and touring. A toe iron with a groove or lip on the side for the cable enabled the cable binding to be used as an uphill binding with free heel, or the cable could be put in the low hitch position for downhill running. New light Kandahar-type bindings of anodized aluminium are now popular in Scandinavia for touring. The Tempo binding made in Norway, has side springs and is also an excellent touring binding.

Figure 10.11 Woodcut from 1870 shows returning hunters. Note the extreme length of these skis.

Just as bindings evolved in response to the steeper alpine terrain, so did poles. Although Zdarsky used only one pole, there is evidence in Switzerland in the 1880s of the use of two poles and they gradually gained increasing popularity. Poles in the Alps, and in the German hills, tended to be much shorter than any in the Scandinavian countries since they were used mostly for going uphill. The Swiss short poles were referred to as "Swagger Sticks".

Meanwhile, in Scandinavia, Norwegian cross-country racers came up with a totally new binding, a one hundred percent toe binding, leaving the heel entirely free. Lauritz Bergendahl, a famous racer and winner at Holmenkollen, is usually credited with the invention. Two cast bronze toe-irons, hinged at the sides, had a lip that pressed down on the sole edge when the jaws were drawn together by a strap. The base plate contained a number of sharp points that penetrated the shoe sole. Originally, small brass posts, or studs, $\frac{1}{4}$ inch in diameter entered holes bored in the shoe. The Bergendahl was the popular racing binding from about 1910 until 1930, and it enabled the Norwegian racers to far surpass the Swedes in the first Olympic Games at Chamonix in 1924. In 1929, the Rotefella (rat trap) and its refinements and adapations supplanted it as a racing binding. It is now widely used for touring on flat land. Even in Norway, Bergendahl bindings were rarely used for touring and today, a heelstrap-type binding, refinements of the Kandahar and Tempo cable bindings, are used for more mountainous terrain as they enable the skier to get a tight fit on the heelstrap.

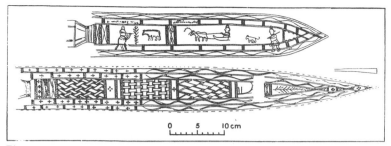

Figure 10.12 Ornamented children's skis made by Lapps. Length 1.34 metres. From **Vasterbotten,** Sweden, 1870.

Figure 10.13 Viennese woodcut of 1890. From **Schneeschuhlaufer**

Figure 10.14 A Norwegian Infantry Regiment drilling on skis, 1892

In Scandinavia, poles underwent some evolution in response to the differing terrains of each country. In the 1920s, the Finns and Swedes developed very long poles, higher than the head. There were no wrist straps. Instead, there was an oval section, so that, when the leather wrapped ends were grasped, the curved spike was headed toward the rear. In Norway, poles named the Torgerson's "Racer Star" were developed which were shorter (shoulder height) and which had straight spikes. They were made of reasonably heavy bamboo, over 1 inch in diameter, and the baskets were very large, approximately 8 inches in diameter, and were made of rattan and rawhide. These adaptations were useful to the more rugged Norwegian terrain and its softer snow.

The skis adopted by the Telemarken natives in the 1860s remained relatively unchanged for more than 50 years. And, in the early days, all skis were designed so that the upturn of the front tip was very gradual. This had two advantages. First, in breaking trail, the tip did not plow the snow, but slipped easily through it and over it.

Figure 10.15 Fridtjof and Eva Nansen from **Life and Explorations of Fridtjof Nansen**

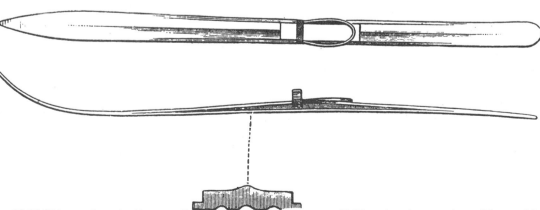

Figure 10.16 Skis used on the Nansen Expedition. This ski measured 2.30 metres long and was 80mm wide at the binding and 92mm wide at the shovel. From **The First Crossing of Greenland.**

Secondly, in case of striking an object, such as a hidden rock or stump beneath the snow surface, or colliding with a tree, the tip did not break, but the shock was transmitted longitudinally along the length of the ski to the foot. In Norway, skis were made of solid hickory; in Sweden and Finland, they were of solid birch; while the German-Austrian-Swiss skis were made of solid ash. In North America, skis were made of birch, maple, basswood, ash and even cherry. In comparison to modern cross-country skis, they all seem heavy and wide.

In the 1930s, alpine ski equipment and cross-country ski equipment really began to diverge in development. Progress in downhill technique lead to alpine boots becoming stiffer and heavier; quite unsuitable for touring. Alpine skis began to be made with a sharp upturn in front which was suitable for use on packed slopes, but poor for touring because such a tip

Figure 10.18 The Ellesfen Shortening Clamp. Still in use today on the Tempo Binding.

plows the snow and is easily broken. In addition, steel edges were built into alpine skis for more control on ice and packed slopes. Meanwhile, cross-country boots became lighter and softer, and new construction techniques using high strength glues and laminations enabled skis to be lightened in weight and narrowed in width.

In 1936, the schism between downhill and Nordic skiing was marked when downhill and slalom racing were added to the Winter Olympics as "Alpine" events. Since then, the prime thrust of interest in skiing occurred in the Alpine events and there was less and less interest in cross-country competition and especially in recreational cross-country skiing or touring. For this reason, during the late 1930s and in the post war years into the 1950s, cross-country touring equipment for recreational purposes was virtually unavailable in North America. This situation has only changed in the last 5 or 6 years.

Figure 10.19 The Bergendahl Binding was the binding that allowed Norwegians to dominate competitive skiing from 1910-1930.

Figure 10.17 Early sole binding. The boot is strapped to a heavy canvas sole which is in turn securely fastened to the ski only at the toe.

Figure 10.20 Dr. Willard B. Soper of Saranac Lake, New York executes a flawless telemark, ca. 1918.

Competitive cross-country skiing in North America has not attracted significant support from the public or large numbers of skiers. Competition has been largely dominated by visiting Norwegians, Swedes or Finns, and outstanding performances by Americans or Canadians are few and far between. Notable are Oliver Perry-Smith, an American who won the German Championship in 1909 and placed second to Bergendahl in the combined during the Saxon Championships of 1913. John Bauer, also an American, won the coveted Holmenkollen Championship in 1956, an unheard of feat for an American skier in modern times. With the new popularity of cross-country skiing, however, we can look forward to future generations so far more competitive skiers. Indeed, the American, Bill Koch performed beautifully at the 1976 Winter Olympics winning a silver medal in the 30 km race. The Frith sisters of Canada have also done well in international competition.

CHRONOLOGY

Pre-Historic

B.C.

3000-2000 Norwegian Rock Paintings depicting Skiers. cf. Paintings of Island of Rödöy.

3000- 500 Skis and ski remnants identified in Nordic moorlands. Most found in Sweden and Finland, about 60 in Norway. Hoting ski.

A.D.

500 The monk Jordanes in his book "De Origine Actibusque Gotarum", mentions the Finnish Laps on skis.

618 Skiing by the Kirghiz mentioned in the annals of the Chinese Tang Dynasty.

770 circa Paulus Diakonus characterized the Finns on account of their skill in skiing, as "Skrid-Finnen", or (Glide-Finns.)

880 Description of a skiing trip at the Julfest (Christmas Feast) in the "Norwegian Royal Tales".

1000 Skiing considered one of the Knightly Skills.

1199 Danish historian Saxo described how ski-runners wage war in Finnmarken, north Finland. (Saxo Grammaticus)

1200 Battle near Oslo in which King Sverre sent men on skis on reconnaisance.

1250 Extraordinary deeds on skis by Nordic people are depicted, mainly in connection with hunting; "Konigspiegel".

1520 Escape and return on skis of Gustav Vasa.

1555 Olaus Magnus, Swedish Archibishop, described in his book "Historia de Gentibus Septentrionalibus", written in exile about his travels in Norway, in which ski-running of the Norwegians is pictured in detail as a common means of travel, in hunting and in competition.

1590 600 Finnish peasants on skis defeat invading Russian troops on the Karelian Isthmus.

1644 Two editions of the book by the Danish historian Saxo appeared which contained the first drawing of a ski.

1675-1679 Norwegian skiers defeat Swedish dragoons in the "Gyldenlovefende" (Battle) at Tröndelagen.

18th Century

1713 "Exercise for a Company of Skiers on their Skis." Book of regulations for Norwegian Ski Companies by Sargaent Emahusen.

1718 In the Swedish-Norwegian War whole ski Battalions appear for the first time.

1767 Advertisement for military-sportive competitions, with money awards, in Kristiania, Norway.

1774 The first winter manoeuver regulations for ski-runners in the Norwegian Army.

1794 The gymnast Vieth refers to the use of skis in his "Encyclopedia for Gymnastics".

19th Century

1804 First German instructions on use of skis in the book; "Gymnastics for Youth", by Gutsmuths.

1809 The Norwegian soldier, Nils Haugo, skis 180 km from Vraadel to Kristiansand in three days.

1831 General Bierch attempted to revive ski-sport in Norway, which had been totally forgotten for decades.

1843 First public race in Tromsö, Norway, which was won by the Finns.

1850s Invention of first modern bindings by Sondre Norheim.

1856 Snowshoe Thompson (born Jon Torsteinson Rui) from Telemark, began his job of transporting mail in a 50 lb. sack by skis across the Sierra Nevada Mountains.

He accomplished the ninety mile mountain journey in an average of 3 days. Thompson carried mail for 20 years.

1861 Norwegian miners, riding skis fashioned from fevee pilings and using single poles, staged their first downhill race at Kiandra, a gold mining town, 45 miles from Canberra, Australia.

1863 First exhibition of types of skis in Trondjhem. (48 pairs of skis)

1865 General Wergeland published his important book on ski-running, in which he refers to it in relation to military history.

1866 First Telemark Regional Jumping Championship in Hoydalsmo. Norheim won.

1868 Inauguration of annual ski-jumping competition in Kristiania. Norheim won.

1870 The Pioneer Ski Club of Australia, formerly called the Kiandra Snow Shoe Club, was founded in 1870 making it one of the oldest ski clubs in the world.

1873 The Nansen Ski Club in Berlin was formed.

1879 Opening of new Ski Jump, Huseby Hill, Kristiania. Men from Telemark demonstrate how to jump.

1881 First Ski School established in Kristiania.

1883 Founding of the Model Ski Association in Kristiania. This association organized competitions at Huseby, and then from 1892 onwards, at Holmenkollen.

1883 Dr. Herwig in Davos makes first trial of Norwegian skis.

1889	First ascent of the Feldberg in the Black Forest by French consulate secretary Pilet, from Mannheim.
1889	The sportsman Klinoschegg tries skis for the first time in Graz.
1889	Norwegian explorer, Fridjot Nansen makes his crossing of Greenland on skis.
1890	Publication of Nansen's book; *"First Crossing of Greenland"*, which was immediately translated into French, English and German and very widely read.
1890	Capt. Vorwerg undertakes the first ski tour in the Riesengebirge.
1891	Founding of the first German Ski Club in Todtnau, in the Black Forest.
1891	A hunting company of a Russian-Siberian division goes 700 km in 10 days on skis under very difficult weather conditions.
1892	Founding of Austrian Ski Association in Vienna.
1893	Establishment of the first Swiss Ski Club.
1893	First use of skis on an alpine tour, conquering the Gotthard, Grimsel and Furka by members of the Ski Club of Todtnau.
1895	Founding of Black Forest Ski Club.
1896	Founding of the first Ski Union in the Riesengebirge. (Sec. 1 of the Austrian Ski Association in the high Elbe)
1897	Publication of *"Alpine Ski-Technique"*; Instructions for Self-Study, by Matthias Zdarsky of Austria.
1897	Traversing on skis of the Bernese Oberland by Wilhelm Paulcke of Germany, followed by the publication of his book *"Ski Running"* in 1899.

20th Century

1900	Founding of the first (sic) North American Ski Club in Ishpeming, Michigan.
1901	First Ski School given by Matthias Zdarsky in the Austrian Alps.
1903	Founding of the Swiss Ski Union
1903	Establishment of Montreal Ski Club, Canada.
1904	The first ascent of Mont Blanc on skis by Hugo Myhuis.
1904	Publication of Richardson's *"Ski-Running"*.
1904	Founding of Ski Club in Vosges.
1905	Founding of Central European Ski Union
1906	Publication of Hoek-Richardson's book *"The Ski"*.
1907	First Austrian Ski Competition at Kitzbühel. Won by Hugo Myhuis.
1908	Founding of the Norwegian Ski Union.
1909	First Finnish Ski Competition.
1910	First International Ski Conference in Kristiania.
1911	Norwegian explorer Roald Amundsen discovers the South Pole. Skis play a vital role in the expedition.
1918-1919	H. Smith (Jack Rabbit) Johannsen of Canada, climbs Mts. Marcy, McIntyre, Whiteface and Haystack in the Adirondacks on skis.
1922	First Winter Games in Garmish-Partenkirchen.
1924	First Winter Olympic Games in Chamonix.
1924	Foundation of International Ski Federation (FIS).
1931	First FIS race in Germany.
1936	Slalom and Downhill racing added to the Winter Olympics.
1943	First public announcement in a newspaper of a Norwegian Ski Race in Tromso.
1961	Founding of the Central Union for the promotion of skiing in Kristiania, whereby use of skis for sport was given further attention.
1976	Bill Koch is the first American to place in Olympic Cross-Country skiing. Awarded the Silver Medal in the 30 km Race at Innsbruck.

GLOSSARY OF TERMS

Alpine Skiing: Downhill and slalom race events as well as downhill recreational skiing; as opposed to Nordic or cross-country skiing.

Anorak: Wind parka of lightweight material, usually with a hood, that is worn over sweaters or down parkas, etc.

Backslip: When the kicking foot in the diagonal stride slips back due to improper wax.

Bail: Clamping device which fits around the boot upper and presses down the sole over the pins of the normal pin binding.

Balaclava: Heavy wool knit cap which covers the entire head to the top of the shoulders with a face hole. Can be folded up and worn as a conventional toque.

Base: Pine tar or pine tar derivative coating that is burned onto the bottoms of all wood skis before waxing.

Base Wax: Wax applied beneath the surface (or running) wax, on the base to improve adhesion.

Basket: Ring at base of ski pole to prevent it from penetrating the snow excessively.

Biathlon: A relay cross-country race and rifle shooting competition.

Binding: Device for fastening ski boot to ski, once called the "harness".

"Bite": Purchase or grip provided by a good wax during the kick phase of the stride.

Bivouac: An emergency or unexpected overnight stop.

Brynje: Net type underwear.

Cagoule: A long knee length anorak especially suitable for foul weather.

Camber: The bend built into all skis to make the pressure on the snow more uniform.

Carabiner: A snap link of light alloy metal which allows the mountaineer to clip in or out of ice screws, chest harness, etc.

Climbing Skins: Fur covered straps tailored to fit the bottom of the ski for use as an aid in climbing.

Combined: Nordic skiing event composed of the best performance in a 15 kilometer cross-country race and a 60 meter jumping competition.

Corn Snow: Wet granular snow associated with Spring conditions.

Dubbin: Boot grease for waterproofing.

Edge: To angle one's skis into the hill to prevent them from slipping sideways down the fall line or to effect a turn.

Fall Line: A line directly down the hill, the shortest distance to the bottom.

Fanny Pack: A belt pack.

Frostnip: Mild surface frostbite which occurs in areas of naturally poor circulation in the skin, such as earlobes, nostrils, etc.

Glide: Amount of free slide which the skier obtains on his forward or riding ski during his stride.

Glissade: Sliding on one's feet and using a pole or poles for a brake. In mountaineering, an ice axe is used.

Groove: Depression in the bottom of the ski to make it run straight and not wander left or right.

Grundvalla: A base material or pine tar derivative.

Grundvox: A base wax.

Heel: The tail or trailing edge of ski.

Kick: Push of rear leg during the stride when the weight is being transferred totally to the gliding ski.

Lignostone: Compressed beechwood which has been impregnated with a phenolic compound. Used for edges of hickory ski bottoms.

Mink Oil: A waterproofing compound suitable for oil tanned leather.

Nordic: Cross-country racing events and jumping events. Recreational cross-country skiing as opposed to downhill skiing.

Orienteering: A sport combining map and compass reading skills with skiing or dry land running.

Pin Binding: A toe-only type binding having pins or studs which project into holes in the sole of the boot.

Pole Plant: Sticking the poles or a pole into the snow at a precise location and instant in time.

Pop-Up: A rubber or spring metal device fastened to the top of the ski under the heel of the boot to prevent ice and snow buildup, it "pops up" when the heel is raised.

Prussik Sling: A continuous loop of rope which can be tied to the climbing rope using a prussik knot to form a step to carry the skier's weight when he is hanging on the rope. The prussik knot can be slid along the rope to enable him to ascend.

Relay: A team race where only one skier skis at a time, tagging another team member for his start of the next leg upon his own finish.

Running: Traveling on skis while utilizing the diagonal stride or other technique to maximize speed.

Scree: Fine talus slope.

Shell: A lightweight nylon parka.

Shortening Clamp: A hinge device in a cable binding which clamps the cable tight by shortening its length. Used in the "Tempo" and "Kandahar" bindings.

Side Camber: The taper of the ski when seen from above. Wider in front than at the back so that the latter tends to track in a straight line behind the tip.

Slip Pass: When the trailing ski in the telemark turn slips behind the boot of the forward ski, causing one's legs to become crossed and an immediate and usually unavoidable fall.

Sole: The bottom of the ski.

Stride: A skier's sliding pace and the basic technique which enables him to progress efficiently.

Surface Wax: Running wax applied on the surface of the ski bottom which comes in direct contact with the snow.

Tail: The trailing edge or rear of the ski, also called the 'heel'.

Talus Slope: A slope covered with loose rock debris from the cliffs overhead. Very slow walking.

Telemark: A steered downhill turning manoeuver requiring touring equipment.

Tip: The leading point or front of the ski.

Tonkin Cane: Bamboo grown in Indo China, used for ski poles.

Torch: A propane, butane, or gasoline blow torch used for "burning in" wax on the ski bottom.

Track: The trail left by skis in soft snow or a prepared racing trail. For the latter, the ski tracks are best seven inches apart on the inside.

"Track!": The call of one skier to another when he wishes him to move aside and allow him to pass.

Traverse: To cross a slope away from the fall line while either ascending or descending.

Toque: A small cap for the head usually of wool and usually stretchable like a sock.

Wands: Small bamboo garden stakes with a flag attached for marking a trail in poor conditions of visibility.

Wedeln: Tail "wagging" or "fish tailing" one's skis in a series of tight incomplete turns.

REFERENCES

Following is a list of useful reference texts available to the reader:

History

Amundsen, K. Vilh, 1923: *Skiløpning* (Ski-Running) Idraetsboken III 1-224 Aschehoug & Co. Kristiania

Bilgeri, O. 1911: *Der Alpine Skilauf* Munich.

Caulfield, Vivian 1911: *How to Ski/Skiing Turns* Scribners, New York (1923)

Dudley, Charles M. 1935: *60 Centuries of Skiing,* Stephen Doye Press, Brattleboro, Vermont.

Huitfeldt, Fritz 1890: *Lehrbuch des Skilaufens* Berlin

Lunn, Arnold 1920: *Cross-Country Skiing* Methuen, London.

Lunn, Arnold 1920: *Skiing for Beginners*

Lunn, Arnold, 1927: *A History of Skiing* Oxford University Press

Lunn, Arnold 1931: *The Complete Ski-Runner* Scribners, New York

Nansen, F. 1890: *First Crossing of Greenland* (Paa Ski Over Gronland) London

Richardson, E. C. 1910: *The Ski Runner*

Rickmers, W. R. 1910: *Ski-ing for Beginners and Mountaineers* London

Thorington, J. M. 1964: *Oliver Perry-Smith: Profile of a Mountaineer* American Alpine Journal; Vol: 14, pages 99-120

Zdarsky, M. 1896: *Lilienfeld Skilauf Technik* Hamburg

If you are interested in learning more about the history of skiing and seeing a fine collection of early equipment visit:

The National Ski Museum,
457A Sussex Drive, Ottawa, Ontario, Canada.

United States Ski Hall of Fame,
Ishpeming, Michigan 49849
Tel: (906) 486-9281

Western American Skisport Museum,
Boreal Ridge, Interstate 80, California
Contact: Auburn Ski Club
839 N. Center Street, Reno, Nevada 89501

Skimuseet Holmenkollbakken,
Holmenkollen, Oslo 3, Norway

Svenska Skidmuseet,
Västerbottens Museum, 90244 Umeå, Sweden

General Technique

"The Mountaineers", Climbing Committee of: *Mountaineering/The Freedom of the Hills* The Mountaineers, Seattle, Washington 1967

Tokle, A. & Luray, M.: *The Complete Guide to Cross Country Skiing and Touring*

Wahlberg, J. 1970: *Cross-Country Skiing, Touring and Racing* The Swedish Amateur Ski Association, Silva Inc., Montreal

Brady, Michael 1971 *Nordic Touring and Cross-Country Skiing* Dreyer, Oslo

Brady, M. & Kvello, K. 1965 *The Norwegian Training Program, Men's Cross-Country* Norwegian Ski Association, Oslo

Caldwell, J. 1971 *The New Cross-Country Ski Book* The Stephen Greene Press, Brattleboro, Vermont.

C.S.A. Quebec Division 1971: *Enseignement Ski de Fond (Discipline Nordique)* Canadian Ski Association

Casewit, Curtis, 1969: *Ski Racing: Advice by the Experts* Arco, New York

Kjellstrom, B. & Ruskin, W. 1972: *Ski Touring for the Beginner* Silva, LaPorte, Indiana

Lederer, W. J. & Wilson, J. P. 1972 *Complete Cross Country Skiing and Ski Touring* W. W. Norton, New York

Lund, M. 1972: *The Pleasures of Cross-Country Skiing* Flare/Avon, New York

Osgood, W. E. & Hurley 1969: *Ski Touring, An Introductory Guide* Chas. E. Tuttle Co., Rutland, Vermont

Rees, David: *Cross-Country Skiing, Touring and Competition* Copp Clark Publishing Toronto 1975

Ski Touring Council: *Ski Touring Guide,* Ski Touring Council, Troy, Vermont. 13th Edition 1976-'77.

Snow Mechanics

Bentley, W. A.: *Snow Crystals* Dover T 287, 1962

La Chapelle, Edward R.: *A Field Guide to Snow Crystals* Univ. of Washington Press, Seattle and London 1969

La Chapelle, Edward R. *The ABC of Avalanche Safety* Colorado Outdoor Sports Co., Denver, Colo. 1970

Nakaya: *Snow Crystals* Harvard University Press 1954

Winter Camping

Berglund, Berndt: *Wilderness Survival* Modern Canadian Library Toronto 1974

Bridge, Raymond: *The Complete Snow Camper's Guide* Scribners, New York 1973

Orienteering

Kjellstrom, B.: *Be Expert with Map and Compass* Scribners

CREDITS

Photos and Illustrations appearing in this book were obtained from the following sources:

The Author: 1.13, pg 22, 2.13, pg 36, 3.1, 3.2, 3.3, 3.7, 3.10, 3.11, 3.12, 3.13, 3.16, 3.17, 3.18, 3.19, 3.20, 3.21, 3.22, 3.23, 4.2, 4.3, 4.4, 4.10, 4.12, 4.13, 4.14, 5.4, 5.34, 5.52, 6.1, 6.2, 6.6, 8.5, 8.11, 8.13, 9.12, 9.13

Gunnar I. Baldwin 5.50, 5.57

Henry I. Baldwin 2.10, 5.25

Eddie Bauer Ltd. 4.8

Black's Camping International 3.8

Bass Sports Inc. 3.24, 5.24

Boston Museum of Science (I. Kamlish) 8.21

Sig Buchmayr Equipment Catalogue of 1955-56 Season 5.37

John A. M. Budden 5.21

Eastern Mountain Sports Inc. 3.26, 3.27, 8.4, 8.6, 8.7

Engadin Skimarathon 2.8

Marilyn Field-Marsham 5.39

Robert F. George 1.2, 1.16, 4.1, 5.1, 5.58, 5.59, 5.60, 5.61, 5.62, 7.3

Richard N. Gibbons 7.4

Haugen Sports Inc. 3.5, 3.9, 3.15

Thor Jacobsen 8.14, 8.15, 8.17, 8.18, 8.19, 8.20, 9.4

Johannsen Wax 6.10

Landsem Ltd. 3.4

Mate Lenard 1.12, 2.9, 4.6, 5.2, 5.3, 5.5, 5.7, 5.8, 5.11, 5.12, 5.13, 5.17, 5.27, 5.32, 5.40, 5.44, 5.46, 5.48, 5.49, 5.51, 5.55, 7.2

Bullaty Lomeo 1.1, 5.56

Margesson's Ltd. 8.8, 8.9

Ontario Ministry of Industry and Tourism 1.3, 1.4, 1.5, 1.6, 1.7, 1.8, 1.9, 2.1, 2.2, 2.3, 2.4, 2.5, 2.6, 2.7, 2.14, 5.28, 6.4, 6.8, 6.12, 7.1

Motronic Inc. 9.10

Mountain Paraphernalia 3.6, 3.25

Mountain Equipment Co-op. 1.14

J. R. Noble 9.1, 9.11

Jim Page 7.5

Photo Features Ltd., 4.11

Recreational Equipment Co. 1.15, 3.14, 4.5

Rex Wax Ltd. 6.7, 6.9

Jan Robertson 2.15, pg 102, 6.13, 8.1

SCIA Inc. 6.3

Bonnie Sheppard 5.6, 5.9, 5.10, 5.14, 5.15, 5.16, 5.19, 5.20, 5.22, 5.26, 5.29, 5.31, 5.33, 5.35, 5.38, 5.42, 9.14, 9.15, 9.16, 9.17, 9.18, 9.20

A&T Ski Company 3.7a

The Ski Hut 2.12, 3.28, 8.2

Pa Skidor pg 160

Der Skifahrer 5.41

Dick Sojecki 2.11, 4.7

Conrad Stenton 5.18, 5.30, 5.45, 5.53

Philip Suter 8.12, 8.16, 8.22, 8.23, 9.2, 9.3, 9.6, 9.7, 9.8, 9.19

Swix Wax 6.5, 6.10

Toko Touring Wax 6.10

The Toronto Star 8.10

W. Twyman 5.23, 5.36, 5.47, 5.54

University of Washington 9.5

Uvex Inc. 3.25

Viksi (Canada) Ltd. 4.9